Preventing Burnout and Building Engagement in the Healthcare Workplace

Preventing Burnout and Building Engagement in the Healthcare Workplace

SECOND EDITION

JONATHON HALBESLEBEN

ACHE Management Series

Library of Congress Cataloging-in-Publication Data is on file at the Library of Congress, Washington, DC.
ISBN: 978-1-64055-369-9

The paper used in this publication meets the minimum requirements of American National Standard for Information Sciences—Permanence of Paper for Printed Library Materials, ANSI Z39.48-1984. ∞ ™

Acquisitions editor: Jennette McClain; Manuscript editor: Joe Pixler; Cover designer: James Slate; Layout: PerfectType

Found an error or a typo? We want to know! Please e-mail it to hapbooks@ache.org, mentioning the book's title and putting "Book Error" in the subject line.

For photocopying and copyright information, please contact Copyright Clearance Center at www.copyright.com or at (978) 750-8400.

Health Administration Press
A division of the Foundation of the
   American College of Healthcare Executives
300 S. Riverside Plaza, Suite 1900
Chicago, IL 60606-6698
(312) 424-2800

For Jenn, Alex, Liesl, and Oliver—
my unconditional sources of social support

Contents

Acknowledgments

PROJECTS SUCH AS this one may end up single-authored, but certainly require a significant, unseen group effort to produce. I have many people to thank for assisting me in this endeavor.

My wonderful wife, Jenn, and our children, Alex, Liesl, and Oliver, have had an extraordinarily supportive role in my ability to write and update this book.

My research collaborators over the years have inspired many of the ideas presented in this book. I particularly thank Tony Wheeler (Widener University), Marilyn Whitman (University of Alabama), Mike Buckley (University of Oklahoma), Samantha Paustian-Underdahl (Florida State University), Matt Bowler (Oklahoma State University), Doug Wakefield (University of Missouri), Bonnie Wakefield (University of Missouri), Cheryl Rathert (St. Louis University), and Mike Mumford (University of Oklahoma).

Jennette McClain, Molly Lowe, Joe Pixler, and the staff at Health Administration Press helped to make this a far better book than I could have ever produced alone. Their tireless behind-the-scenes work to produce such high-quality work is admirable.

I especially want to thank the thousands of healthcare professionals who informed this book. I appreciate their candor in sharing their experiences. While the milieu regarding stress has shifted toward accepting that stress is inevitable in healthcare, it still requires a great deal of courage to share and relive the stress in one's life.

Finally, I want to thank you. Because you are reading this book, you recognize that stress and burnout are having an impact on those you work with. More important, it suggests you have the audacity to do something about it! Clearly, you have some hope that you can address the stress problems in your facility. My hope is that, by the end of this book, I have energized that hope so you can tackle the problem head-on. It will be a challenging journey; I'm grateful for the opportunity to be part of it.

The Role of the Healthcare Leader in Addressing Stress and Burnout and Building Engagement

My job has always had its stressful moments. We see all kinds of terrible things here in the ER, but at least we know that in most cases our intervention will help people get through it. In fact, that's what keeps me going. I know I'm making a difference.

—Nurse working in the emergency department of a regional hospital, December 2019

Next Monday is my last day. I've spent more than a year trying to save people who won't help themselves. I've watched colleagues die doing the same. I just can't do it anymore.

—Nurse working in the emergency department of the same regional hospital, May 2021

A BRIDGE INSPECTOR'S WORST NIGHTMARE

A friend of mine is a bridge inspector for a state department of transportation. One day, we got to talking about our jobs and I asked him, "When you think about your work, what is your worst nightmare?" I assumed it would be that he missed something in an inspection that caused a catastrophic collapse, or something like that.

In 2007, about 15 years prior to our conversation, I lived 90 miles east of the Interstate-35W bridge over the Mississippi River near downtown Minneapolis, Minnesota, when it collapsed, resulting in 13 deaths and 145 injuries. Several of my family members lived in the Twin Cities area, and although I knew the odds were very low that they had been on the bridge at that time, I was immediately afraid that they might have been. Images of that scene have been forever seared in my memory.

His response came as something of a surprise. He agreed that, sure, missing something in an inspection would be terrible, particularly if it led to a collapse with loss of life. However, he explained, the bridges at highest risk for catastrophic events are inspected regularly. He also added that the vast majority of bridges he inspects span relatively short lengths at modest heights, so a collapse would certainly be costly and potentially dangerous but likely would not lead to loss of life.

So, what was his worst nightmare?

"Seeing, day after day, the relatively minor stresses on our bridges, reporting the concerns, then seeing those same minor stresses gradually get a little worse each time I inspect the same bridge. The nightmare isn't the individual bridge. It's knowing that the cracks in the system will keep growing, we're not doing enough about that, and eventually the whole system is going to fail."

Sound familiar? When I wrote the first edition of this book in 2009, the systemic concerns about stress and burnout among healthcare professionals were already well known. Worries about staffing shortages were documented and projected to get worse. We were starting to acknowledge that the systems we put in place to make care safer were also, at times, affecting workflow in ways that put added demands on clinicians. There were hints that the supply chain may be a bit more fragile than we might have hoped, too. And we knew that while our population was living longer and serious conditions requiring hospitalizations were on the decline, underlying risk factors of serious illness such as diabetes were gradually increasing over time. Considered together, the cracks in the system were already showing.

People were starting to see the problem. In 2019, the World Health Organization added burnout to the International Disease Classification (ICD-11) as a "syndrome." That same year, the National Academy of Medicine released its groundbreaking report *Taking Action Against Clinical Burnout.* The American Medical Association created its STEPS Forward program in 2015 with training modules on professional well-being. According to several studies, nearly one physician dies by suicide *each day* in the United States (Kalmoe et al. 2019).

Just as my bridge inspector friend feared, we had already identified the risks in the system. Then the COVID-19 pandemic struck, and the stressors were intensified. Since early 2020, we have been faced with an unceasing barrage of heartbreaking stories from healthcare professionals describing a vicious cycle of strain, turnover, staffing shortages, and more strain—all in the context of worrying about their own personal safety when going to work each day.

In the first edition of this book, I tried to convince readers that burnout in healthcare wasn't just a fad or the result of an increased willingness of healthcare professionals to admit they were stressed. I still make the case for why it is important that we address stress and burnout, but I assume by this point you don't need much further convincing. You either are experiencing burnout or observing burnout in your organization and have made the courageous decision to do something about it.

In this, the second edition, I have changed the title to reflect the recent shift in emphasis from reducing stress to building engagement. This may seem to be a subtle change, but it is important to signal that the end goal is engagement.

My intent is to put you as a healthcare leader in a better position to address the stress of those with whom you work in order to foster engagement in their work.

You can't afford to let this problem continue unabated. Not only is addressing burnout the right thing to do for the healthcare professionals you employ, work with, and contract with, it will benefit your organization dramatically in terms of smoother functioning and better bottom-line performance. To get started, let's try to define the ubiquitous concept of *stress* in terms of what it is and what it is not.

WHAT STRESS IS

Part of what makes stress so challenging to address is that, at its root, stress is more difficult to define than one might imagine. It is one of those ideas that people can identify when they see it but would be hard-pressed to pinpoint in words. What started out as a term used by engineers to describe the forces affecting bridges and other structures has evolved into a human phenomenon. Researchers have debated the definition of stress for many years, and a consensus has yet to emerge.

What makes stress so hard to define is a lack of clarity about whether we are talking about a state of being, an event, a process, or something else altogether. For example, when people say they are "stressed," do they mean they are experiencing a state of stress-fulness? Do they mean they have just experienced an acute event that they interpreted as negative? Or do they mean they are using some sort of cognitive process to compare their current situation to their desired situation (and are presumably reaching an unfavorable conclusion)?

The National Institute for Occupational Safety and Health (NIOSH) has been a leading government agency in the study of stress in the United States. In its seminal report *Stress . . . At Work,* NIOSH (1999) defined job stress as "the harmful physical and emotional responses that occur when the requirements of the job do not match the capabilities, resources, or needs of the worker." In a way, NIOSH's definition summarizes the three possibilities noted in the previous paragraph. By including the idea of a response to a stimulus, the definition highlights the cognitive process as well as the acute event (consideration of the requirements of the job).

A critical aspect of NIOSH's definition is the cognitive evaluation that underlies stress. This evaluation has long been a focal point of stress theorists who believe that a simple tally of someone's stressful experiences (which I will refer to as *stressors*) is insufficient to understand how stress is experienced. As a result of this thinking, the life event scales that were popularized early on to determine stress—scales on which you checked off whether you received a promotion, got divorced, got married, had a child, and had a death in the family—have fallen out of favor. We now recognize that our reactions to these events, rather than the events themselves, are potentially more problematic.

In summary, stress is a state of being that results from our evaluation of a specific situation. It is our response when we face a demand at work or in other aspects of our life but do not feel we have sufficient resources to meet the demand.

WHAT STRESS IS NOT

In addition to defining what stress is, it may also be helpful to clarify what stress is not. A number of constructs are similar to stress, and indeed related to stress, but should not be confused for stress. We will turn our attention here to *dissatisfaction* and *incompetence*.

Stress Is Not Dissatisfaction

Stress is not the same as dissatisfaction with work. Someone highly satisfied with their work could be stressed because they spend so much time worrying about aspects of their job. Positive, satisfying events at work (e.g., promotions) can also be stressful.

Over time, stress can lead to dissatisfaction. As stress mounts, people will eventually react negatively to it. Most people expect some level of stress in their jobs, but when it seems inescapable or when it seems like it could have been avoidable, they are likely to reach a point where they become dissatisfied with the job.

Stress Is Not Incompetence

People who experience stress aren't incompetent. If not carefully considered, the NIOSH definition might lead one to that conclusion (e.g., the requirements of the job don't meet the capabilities of the worker). However, one also needs to consider the rest of the definition—"the needs of the worker *and* [emphasis added] the resources available to the worker." The person might be highly capable of doing their job but does not find that it meets their needs. They may not be earning enough and thus cannot meet their material needs. Or, the job might not be providing the psychosocial stimulation they seek. Under these circumstances, even a competent person may experience a great deal of stress.

The definition also cites insufficient resources to meet the requirements of the job. I'll define *resources* more carefully later in the book, but for now, I'll just say that resources can include nearly anything—time, financial support, assistance from colleagues, equipment, and so forth—that can help a person manage the demands of their work. This problem is readily apparent to many healthcare professionals: They would like to spend more time with each of their patients, but staffing crunches have increased the number of patients assigned to them. As result, they feel as though they are not meeting the requirements of the job, at least to the extent they would like to meet them. Again, the issue is not one of incompetence. They just do not have the resources they need to meet the demands.

THE STRESS PARADOX

One of the difficulties in addressing stress is something I refer to as the *stress paradox:* For the most part, stress processes are personal, subjective experiences. However, when we want to reduce stress, individual interventions are not particularly effective. Why is that so? The answer to that question is key to this book. If we can understand why individuals uniquely experience stress (for example, why one colleague thrives on short deadlines while another finds them debilitating) and why individual interventions don't work, we will move much closer to addressing the problem of stress in the workplace. In this introduction, I'll outline the basic arguments for the stress paradox as a way to present the assumptions on which this book is built.

Everyone Experiences Stress, but Not Everyone Experiences Burnout

We know that stress is an individual experience. As a result, while we all experience stress, we do not all experience the intense strain that characterizes burnout. *Burnout* is an extreme response to work stress that occurs when we continually face stressors with which we are unable to fully cope. Most, if not all, people will react at some point to stressors by concluding that they don't have adequate resources. However, the percentage of people who would be characterized as burned out is lower. Some people are able to deal with the stressors in life and can stop them from becoming so bad that they burn out. If some people can mitigate stress themselves, don't we have all the more reason to treat stress individually? On the surface, this logic seems sound, but let's dig a little deeper.

The Commonality of Stressors

Although the experience of stress varies from person to person, we still find remarkable consistency among the variation. When surveys are conducted in departments or common work areas (e.g., a floor in a hospital), the stressors that people name are frequently the same. The degrees of burnout also tend to be highly consistent within groups of coworkers. Thus, while people may react somewhat differently to the stressors, employees working together typically react negatively to the same stressors.

For example, when staffing is a problem, it is a problem for everyone. Treating this problem individually won't work. Imagine telling a nurse in an intensive care unit (ICU) that the staffing issue is not really that big of a deal and that they should think about it as an opportunity to show their value, or that staffing wouldn't be an issue if they managed their time better. Simply telling someone to reframe the problem won't make it go away, especially if everyone else is observing the same problem. As hard as that nurse might try to think about short staffing as an opportunity, they are still going to struggle to get the work done and are still going to hear about the problem repeatedly.

People Know What Is Causing Their Stress, and They Often Know the Solution, Too

The final assumption of this book, and arguably the key to addressing stress at work, is that employees often know what is causing it. If you approach the subject delicately with them, you'll be able to solicit this information, and if you are smart, you'll ask them how they would fix the situation.

Countless well-intentioned stress management programs have failed because managers thought they knew what was causing stress in the workplace and then came up with a flashy solution. These managers may have wanted to show off their expertise and leadership ability, or perhaps they didn't want to bother their employees by soliciting their feedback. More likely, they did so because they (1) feared what they might discover and (2) feared that their employees would come up with solutions that they, as the manager, could not implement.

Hopefully, this book will convince you that such thinking is extremely problematic and is actually contributing further to the problem of stress in healthcare. Among other factors, burnout frequently occurs when employees experience stress and feel very little control over it. Giving employees a voice in the matter provides them with a sense that they can help to address this problem—not just for themselves, but for others as well.

What's particularly powerful is that such a process doesn't just help reduce burnout, it also creates the conditions for employees to be more engaged in their work. As I will outline in this book, an engaged workforce of health professionals is a very powerful force not only in improving the care environment but also in preventing stress from becoming burnout. As we will discuss, involving employees is among the most crucial processes to building employee engagement.

That last point places some of the responsibility for addressing stress on your employees, since I will advocate strongly for their involvement in the process. But don't underestimate your role in solving the problem. Employees may have the solutions but wait for someone to ask about them. They will need your help in developing detailed action plans and securing the resources necessary to implement potential solutions. You will help build the framework that allows for long-term sharing of ideas and implementation of those ideas.

WHAT'S NEW IN THIS EDITION

This edition includes important changes from the first. Of course, I've incorporated current research and new ideas that have been tested out in healthcare organizations since the previous edition. I've incorporated more dramatic updates, too.

The topic of employee engagement was discussed in the previous edition; however, that topic has grown in importance in the intervening years for researchers and managers. I suppose one could argue that just reducing stress and burnout in healthcare professions would be progress, but we are now seeing that organizations simply cannot be competitive without an engaged workforce. As a result,

I've added a full chapter on engagement to outline the way it is conceptualized, how employees can be engaged, and the benefits of an engaged workforce. I have also expanded coverage of the final step in the BRIDGES program—*sustain*—to emphasize that building an organization that has engaged employees is perhaps the best way to sustain your progress in reducing stress and burnout.

In the time since the first edition was published, another major force has played a role in healthcare: the COVID-19 pandemic. As I am working on this book, we are now more than three years into a pandemic that few thought would last this long or have such an impact. The pandemic has exacerbated some of the most significant sources of stress and burnout in healthcare organizations while introducing a host of new stressors. In this edition, I have tried to draw out some of the lessons we have learned from the pandemic with the hope that, at least when it comes to health and well-being of healthcare professionals, we might be better prepared for the next significant disruption.

PLAN FOR THE BOOK

This book will lead you to a better position to address the stress you and your employees face regularly. To that end, we'll start by making the business case for addressing stress. I will convince you that not dealing with stress is far more costly than addressing it head-on. We'll explore why people in healthcare experience so much stress and burnout and then identify sources of that stress. We'll focus on burnout because it represents the point at which the stress becomes debilitating. We'll also introduce the notion of employee engagement as the outcome of people who have the resources necessary to deal with the demands of their work. From there, we will discuss strategies for reducing burnout that employees—and you—are experiencing now, for preventing future burnout, and for building engagement.

By the conclusion of the book, you will be in a better position to help your employees reverse their burnout and then to fully engage them in their work.

CHAPTER 1

Making the Case for Addressing Stress and Burnout and Pursuing Engagement in Healthcare Organizations

I realized on day one that my job was going to be more stressful than I had anticipated. For a while I tried to deal with it, to cope, I guess. But after a few months, I just couldn't take it anymore.

—Former physical therapist in a community hospital, now an insurance claims representative

I was burned out. I would show up to work but was completely checked out. I know I wasn't as careful as I should have been and probably made some pretty bad mistakes. It sounds bad, but I just didn't care.

—Pharmacist in an academic medical center

WHY YOU NEED TO CARE ABOUT STRESS AND BURNOUT AMONG YOUR STAFF

Stress is an easy thing to ignore. It seems normal. Everyone is stressed, right? If you aren't a little stressed, are you really doing your job? In some ways, the answer to both questions is yes. Even the earliest stress theorists and researchers concluded that some degree of stress (or perhaps better framed as "arousal") was required to accomplish daily activities. In fact, our mere state of wakefulness means that we are experiencing stress.

However, we also know that too much stress can cause problems. In this chapter, I will review the significant impact that stress can have on healthcare professionals and administrative staff. In doing so, I will make a business case for caring about stress among healthcare staff. My goal isn't to tug at your heartstrings by arguing that a caring manager needs to worry about how stressed their staff is. That might be true, but there is also a very real cost associated with stress and burnout. For better or worse, leading healthcare organizations are more likely to pay attention to the financial argument. I am convinced that after I lay out these consequences, you will also be convinced that stress and, in its extreme form, burnout are issues that you need to strongly consider because of the impact on both your heartstrings and your purse strings.

COMMON CONSEQUENCES OF STRESS AMONG HEALTHCARE PROFESSIONALS

I hesitate to lump clinical and administrative professionals together when sorting out the negative impact of stress. As outlined in the introduction, not everyone experiences stress in the same way. Moreover, as discussed in chapter 2, the sources of stress vary according to the type of clinical work. However, when we study the impact of stress on the working professional, we see that the patterns are remarkably consistent across occupations.

Burnout Leads to Lower Performance

One of the more consistent findings in the literature is that stress, especially when it reaches the point of burnout, has a negative impact on job performance. Performance is considered a multiplicative function of one's ability and motivation. In other words, to perform a job, one must have both the ability (e.g., the requisite skills and knowledge) and motivation to do the job. Stress and burnout tend to have a greater impact on the motivation side of the equation. When employees are burned out, they generally retain the ability to do the work but their desire to complete the work markedly declines. Consider the implications of this finding for a moment: We have a workforce that can do the job but has little desire to do it. What a waste of human potential!

The underlying reason for the lack of motivation is essentially a resource allocation problem. In the introduction, I suggested that stress results from a mismatch between the demands of the job and the resources available to meet those demands. When we face demands at work, we allocate some of our resources to meet each new demand we face. For example, when a new patient is transferred to a floor, the nurses on that floor have a new set of demands on their time, skills, material resources, and even physical energy (in terms of burned calories). We repeatedly make decisions about how we will allocate or invest our resources.

What we tend to find is that people allocate their resources strategically, though that strategy is typically focused on short-term avoidance of further loss. When we are less burned out, we may not think twice about helping another employee who seems to be having trouble. We may take a little more time to double-check our work (e.g., check a medication order twice to make sure the dosage is correct). But as our stress increases to the point where our resources are severely diminished, we naturally allocate our resources more carefully. Suddenly, we're not sure whether we have the time to help that colleague—unless we determine that doing so may benefit us soon after offering the help (i.e., we believe the colleague will reciprocate).

Burnout Affects How Work Gets Done

This resource allocation process has important implications for how work gets done in healthcare organizations. Over the years,

I've conducted a number of research studies on the concept of work-arounds—creative solutions for addressing blocks in work-flow. It will come as little surprise that healthcare professionals are constantly dealing with blocks as they go about their work. Supplies are not available because supply chain issues persist, patients' charts are missing information, or medication orders are not properly filled. Some of these blocks may be intentional, such as the forcing functions embedded in bar code medication administration technologies that make the employee stop and think about what they are doing. But most of the blocks are not intentional; they are, instead, problems with work design or coordination.

However, when an employee is burned out, these blocks are interpreted differently. For example, scanning the medication and armband in a bar code medication administration system is not a big deal when stress is low. But in the face of burnout, a nurse might feel that the task is inconvenient and taking up valuable time. Some nurses make copies of the patient armbands and place them close to the medications to eliminate repeated trips to the bedside for scanning. This shortcut saves them time as they administer medications, but it also eliminates the safety advantage that was built into the bar code system.

We researchers have applied this idea not only to patient safety, but also to the safety of the healthcare professional. In the same way that nurses (and other professionals) may work around patient safety features, they may shortcut safety procedures meant to protect themselves. We find that when nurses experience higher levels of burnout, they engage in risky practices such as not asking for assistance when moving patients. As a result, they increase their possibility of incurring occupational injuries such as musculoskeletal damage.

Taken together, our work (e.g., Halbesleben, Rathert, and Williams 2013; Rathert et al. 2012) suggests that when stress mounts, healthcare professionals focus their resources in ways that allow them to get the tasks done in the moment but don't have the resources to consider the underlying issues that led them to have to create work-arounds. As a result, that may suboptimize their outcomes.

If they are reallocating their resources repeatedly, they may come to feel that they are not a good fit for the job.

Burnout Leads to Higher Turnover

Turnover, and particularly thinking about turnover, is the next potential consequence. Burnout is strongly linked to negative consequences such as job dissatisfaction, lower commitment, and eventual turnover. A recent analysis of more than 50,000 registered nurses in the United States found that of those who left their organizations, 31.5 percent reported leaving because of burnout (Shah et al. 2021). High levels of stress are shocks to an employee's system. What is interesting is that the stress, and the resulting shocks, lead them to focus less on the issues with their work that caused the stress and more on whether they should continue in the job or profession where they experience the stress.

Most healthcare professionals have spent a significant amount of time training for their professions. While that training might be stressful, it is typically completed with the idea that it will pay off in the end. When they take that job and realize that their expectations are not met, those professionals may start to wonder whether they took the wrong job or whether they took the wrong career path altogether. As a result, they start thinking about other options and may even begin a job search.

This effect appears to be particularly pronounced among early careerists (especially first-year professionals) and may explain why more than a quarter of nursing turnover occurs in the first year (Nursing Solutions, Inc. 2022). If someone is really burned out, they are unlikely to stick around for a long time. In many healthcare professions, this factor had already contributed to the well-documented staffing shortages before the COVID-19 pandemic. The perfect storm of baby boomers' retirement, high early-career turnover, and inadequate capacity in training programs had created a crisis in most healthcare professions—and the pandemic was gasoline added to the fire, exacerbating already-known issues. In many ways, the pandemic created the ultimate shock for many healthcare professionals. The broader issue of the psychological processes leading to turnover is beyond the scope of this book; however, research consistently finds a relationship between high levels of stress and turnover across occupations.

Burnout Is Harmful to Health

A growing body of literature supports the idea that job stress is negatively associated with health. As this research becomes more popular and more sophisticated, the findings are revealing that stress, particularly when it reaches the point of burnout, has a greater impact on occupational health than initially realized. Researchers have consistently linked stress and burnout to negative health outcomes, including cardiovascular disease, lower-rated self-health, type 2 diabetes, and male infertility.

The link between stress and health outcomes is not necessarily direct. Instead, there are various intervening processes, both physiological and behavioral, at work. Stress can affect development of areas of the brain that support stress responses (Hambrick, Brawner, and Perry 2019). Further, stress activates an autonomic response involving our neuroendocrine and immune systems, and those responses are commonly associated with sleep disturbances (Demichelis et al. 2022).

As studies have shown, another way of connecting stress with negative health outcomes is to look at problematic behaviors that people use to cope with stress. Examining a data set of nearly 3,000 people, Jackson and colleagues (2010) found that stress was associated with overeating and substance use, particularly for people in already-challenging environments that made these forms of coping easily available. In view of this data, the link between stress and symptoms of diabetes and cardiovascular disease is not surprising.

Burnout can also lead to injuries while engaging in some of the work-arounds I mentioned earlier. Findings from some of my published research suggest that burned-out nurses and sonographers are more likely to engage in work-arounds related to safety equipment and procedures that are meant to protect them. As a result, they are more likely to be injured on the job. One would hope that would prompt those health professionals to reduce their work-arounds, going back to the processes as they were intended. However, what I found is that those injuries lead them to be even more burned out and even more likely to engage in safety work-arounds.

Consequences of Stress and Burnout for Healthcare Professionals

- Decreased performance
- Problematic (even dangerous) adjustments to work processes
- Higher turnover
- Poorer health

Vicious Cycles

As if these consequences weren't enough, emerging research suggests that people who are burned out tend to enter a vicious cycle that worsens their burnout over time. The idea is pretty straightforward: As our resources are depleted, we are left with fewer options for investing our remaining resources; thus, we are more likely to lose those resources. For example, if we have barely enough resources to do our job, we are not likely to exhibit extra behaviors that would make us a candidate for promotion. As a result, we are stuck in a job that is draining our resources.

The good news is that we as healthcare leaders can use these cycles to our advantage at times. We can also create *virtuous* cycles if we can attain a critical mass of resources. Employees then can allocate their resources in a way that continually generates new ones. When this model is achieved, the result is a highly engaged workforce.

Burnout from the Healthcare Professional's Perspective

In putting together all the processes mentioned here, a picture emerges that will resonate with a lot of readers. A healthcare professional, regardless of whether they are in a clinical, leadership, or support role, enters the profession with the noble goal of helping others and saving lives. As they start their careers, they realize those outcomes are more difficult than they imagined, which causes stress. To deal with stressors, they make work-arounds that work in the short term but end up causing other problems later. Their physical health starts to deteriorate. Eventually, stress accumulates to the point where they become burned out. They start thinking about whether their organization cares about their well-being and whether there's a better option for them out there. They may even start thinking about whether they are a good fit for their role. In the end, they realize that it is unlikely that they will ever reach their original goals of truly helping people, so they consider an entirely different profession.

All that sounds pretty bad from the perspective of the individual. In the next section, we will explore how that pattern of individual thinking ends up aggregating to create significant problems at the organizational level.

THE IMPACT ON ORGANIZATIONAL PERFORMANCE

The impact that stress makes on organizational performance is less clear. While stress certainly has a marked effect on healthcare professionals as described earlier, research that sorts out the relationships between stress and its effects is difficult to conduct for many reasons. Stress has a delayed effect on organizations. It may build among employees for years until the full cost is realized. Therefore, causal research designs at the organizational level are nearly impossible to implement. However, if we extend our discussion of the impact of stress on individuals, the organizational-level consequences become clear.

We have already made the connection between burnout and outcomes, such as the link between performance and turnover. Lower performance and higher turnover have real costs in terms of human resource losses. The lost productivity associated with lower performance is pronounced. While no figures specific to health-care are available, the American Institute of Stress (2022) estimates workplace stress to cost more than $300 billion in the US economy alone. This figure is largely based on accidents, absenteeism, reduced productivity, medical costs, worker's compensation claims, and other associated costs. Again, while this figure is for the entire United States, a conservative estimate of 15 percent to represent the portion of the economy represented by healthcare would still add up to about $20 billion. Imagine how that money could be used constructively in the healthcare sector.

Turnover

A good bit of that $20 billion comes from costs associated with turnover. When someone quits their job, there are direct costs associated with recruiting and selecting someone to fill the position (e.g., advertising the position, working with a search firm, paying for candidate travel for interviews), training a new person once they take the job, and lost productivity (including lost clinical income, in some cases) resulting from the temporary reduction in staffing and the learning curve for the new hire. These costs don't even include the indirect costs associated with lower morale when someone vacates a position.

The costs associated with turnover vary significantly, depending on the occupation. While the actual cost will vary due to a significant number of factors (e.g., local economy, supply and demand in the profession), the rule of thumb is that the replacement cost is about two times the salary of the employee being replaced. To gain a sense of what turnover is costing your organization, the American Medical Association has created a calculator that specifically refers to physician burnout but could be easily adapted to any profession (https://edhub.ama-assn.org/steps-forward/module/2702510).

The numbers also should be put in a proper perspective based on turnover rates. Although the cost of replacing a nurse may be much lower than for a physician, the overall costs may not be much different because of the higher number of nurses who need to be replaced. A recent NSI report (Nursing Solutions, Inc. 2022) found that the turnover rate for nurses was just under 19 percent. Considering the number of nurses in a facility, the cost to replace each one, and that level of turnover, the report found that the average hospital in the study was losing between $3.6 million and $6.5 million *per year*. Put another way: Just a 1 percent change in turnover can either cost or save a facility upwards of $270,000 a year. One can find similar—even higher—turnover rates for other healthcare occupations such as sonographers.

Of course, we cannot attribute all turnover costs to stress. Turnover happens for any number of reasons including promotion, retirement, or relocation. We cannot eliminate turnover, nor would we want to do so. Turnover can serve a purpose, such as in the case of an employee who doesn't fit the culture or is underperforming. Turnover can also be useful to manage the workforce size when demand or the economy weakens (e.g., using attrition rather than layoffs or terminations to reduce the workforce).

However, the relationship between stress (especially burnout) and turnover is strong. We cannot stop people from retiring, nor can we stop someone's spouse from accepting a job elsewhere. And we certainly wouldn't want to prevent promotions! What we can do, however, is prevent most stress-related turnover.

I can imagine a potential response to these arguments: *If employees can't hack it, why should we prevent their stress? Why not just find someone who can cope?* Unfortunately, some leaders have taken this thinking so far as to use "stress interviewing" to test potential employees' responses to stress. Unfortunately, such approaches rarely yield the intended effect of weeding out potential employees who can't handle stress. That line of thinking also ignores an important reality: There aren't enough healthcare professionals in the labor market as it is, and relying on temporary solutions such as travel registered nurses is extremely costly. In the end, investing in solutions to reduce stress and its associated turnover will almost always be a better long-term investment than dealing with the churn of stressed-out employees in a tight labor market.

The effect of stress on turnover and retention may be even more insidious than I have already described. Two parallel findings from my research are of serious concern. First, when significant events cause people to consider their job situations, the top-performing employees leave their jobs first. And on the other hand, a surprisingly large group of employees would prefer to leave a stressful environment but, for whatever reason, are stuck in their job. Because of their lower productivity, these "stuck" employees may engender just as negative an impact on an organization as the employees who left. I can think of few situations worse than losing top employees to stress while keeping lower-performing employees.

Health-Related Costs

Beyond turnover, there are other human resource costs associated with stress, particularly those directly associated with health. For example, the seminal 2008 report from Higgins and colleagues found that high levels of role overload (a form of stress) are associated with more than $6 billion per year in physician visits, emergency department visits, and inpatient hospital stays in Canada. While these data represent all occupations, they could apply to healthcare professions as well. These findings also indicate a significant burden on healthcare system utilization as a result of stress, which only adds to the stress of healthcare professionals.

A related issue is worker's compensation claims for stress-related issues. Regardless of the legitimacy of such claims, they exist and may be something your organization will face. Even if direct claims of stress in the context of worker's compensation are disallowed, stress may be associated with compensable claims for traditional workplace injuries such as needlesticks and musculoskeletal damage, so it still must be considered a worker's compensation risk.

The relationship between stress and health suggests a link between stress and sickness-related absence from work. Again, this issue is muddy and difficult to sort out. If you catch a cold, you will have difficulty attributing it directly to stress. Regardless, any human resources director will tell you that absences related to sickness have a significant cost. Higgins and colleagues (2008) estimate that absenteeism from work stress creates direct costs of $1 billion per year in Canada. Obviously, such absences are not always preventable, especially in healthcare where exposure to illness is higher than in other industries because of the nature of the work. However, absences resulting from sickness that is indirectly related to stress should decrease if stress is addressed.

Organizational Consequences of Stress and Burnout

- Higher turnover
- Higher healthcare costs

THE IMPACT ON PATIENTS

So far, I have highlighted the direct and indirect costs associated with stress from the perspective of clinical staff, administrative staff, and the organization as a whole. If you aren't convinced yet about the gravity of the issue, try looking at it this way: Stress among your employees significantly affects the quality of care they provide to their patients. It leads to medical errors, near misses, and lower patient satisfaction.

A meta-analysis of data from more than 200,000 healthcare providers in 82 studies found compelling links between burnout and quality of care and safety. (A meta-analysis combines studies of a topic into one big analysis to significantly increase the sample size of the research and enables you to address broader questions.) This particular meta-analysis found that burnout was consistently associated with lower quality care and lower patient safety (Salyers et al. 2017; see also Jun et al. 2021 for a systematic review focused on nurses). Digging deeper, studies are revealing that burnout is associated with higher levels of infection, medical errors, and post-discharge recovery time (Cimiotti et al. 2012; Montgomery et al. 2021; Tawfik et al. 2018).

Of course, some problems with quality of care and safety result from the turnover discussed earlier. An increasing body of evidence suggests that nurse turnover, staffing shortages, and related issues severely affect the quality of patient care. Such research is well established and familiar to most healthcare executives, so let's focus on the other ways that stress can have on patients.

Recent studies suggest that the relationship between burnout and patient outcomes is driven by problems such as less teamwork and lower adherence to infection control protocols (Colindres et al. 2018; de Lima Garcia et al. 2019), both of which require an investment of resources.

The links between burnout and patient safety are growing and startling. While we still cannot attach an exact figure to the number of avoidable medical errors attributable to stress and burnout, the literature supports the idea that there is a relationship between the two.

Research suggests that burned-out healthcare professionals who report medical errors likely see reporting as a necessary resource allocation, or at least realize that the costs of not reporting are simply too high (Halbesleben et al. 2008). However, a growing body of research suggests that they may be less likely to report near misses—that is, instances in which an error did not occur but likely would have if someone had not intervened (Arnetz et al. 2017; Hall et al. 2019). Near-miss reports are typically voluntary, in the sense that no one would know about these events if they weren't reported. As a result, healthcare professionals may see reporting as an extra part of the job and feel that resources should not be allocated for it. Near-miss reports present an extraordinary learning opportunity, but burnout seems to be keeping organizations from learning from them.

One of the more established patient consequences of burnout is lower patient satisfaction. This relationship has been the crux of most burnout outcomes research and is consistently replicated. There is a host of possible mediating factors, such as poor communication, that help to explain this relationship; however, burnout seems to be the point at which problems start.

TAKEAWAY POINTS: THE COST OF STRESS AND BURNOUT TO HEALTHCARE

An absolute dollar figure cannot be placed on the cost of stress and burnout to the healthcare profession. There are too many variables involved and too many connections that have yet to be solidified. The effects of stress are too individualized, context sensitive, and time dependent to be pinned down to a firm figure.

Moreover, although evidence clearly links stress with these serious outcomes, we will never be able to come up with absolute causal links between stress and the outcomes described in this chapter. I doubt many healthcare organizations and their employees would be willing to volunteer for a randomized, controlled trial of stress and outcomes in which one group is randomly assigned to the "high stress group" and observed for such things as lower performance, injuries, turnover, insurance claims, and medical errors.

This impossibility, however, doesn't diminish the main message here: There is a *significant* long-term cost of stress among healthcare professionals. To summarize, here is the straightforward case for why you should be concerned about stress and burnout in your organization:

- Stress and burnout are associated with lower employee performance, turnover, and diminished health.
- As a result, stress and burnout represent significant financial costs to healthcare organizations.
- Stress and burnout also are associated with lower-quality care as a result of medical errors and lower patient satisfaction.
- The negative consequences of stress and burnout are at least partially preventable.

The bottom line is that stress and burnout in healthcare organizations lead to considerable financial and human costs and must be addressed. Of course, to address burnout, we must understand how it develops. We'll turn to that process in the next chapter.

FURTHER READING

Bakhamis, L., D. P. Paul III, H. Smith, and A. Coustasse. 2019. "Still an Epidemic: The Burnout Syndrome in Hospital Registered Nurses." *Health Care Manager* 38 (1): 3–10. https://doi.org/10.1097/HCM.0000000000000243.

Salyers, M. P., K. A. Bonfils, L. Luther, R. L. Firmin, D. A. White, E. L. Adams, and A. L. Rollins. 2017. "The Relationship Between Professional Burnout and Quality and Safety in Healthcare: A Meta-Analysis." *Journal of General Internal Medicine* 32 (4): 475–82. https://doi.org/10.1007/s11606-016-3886-9.

CHAPTER 2

Defining the Problem of Stress and Burnout in Healthcare Organizations

Frustrating.

Frustrating.

Stressful.

Frustrating and stressful.

—Responses of four nurses in a community hospital intensive care unit when asked about the personal impact of making constant adjustments because of poor work design

I reached a point where I'd walk into the room and I wouldn't even acknowledge the patient. I'd ask the resident or nurse what was going on, look over the chart, and bark out an order. The patients were a problem that needed solving, not people.

—An attending physician on a cardiac intensive care unit

HOW DID WE GET SO STRESSED OUT?

In this chapter, I am going to describe theories about how healthcare professionals experience stress and how that stress can lead to burnout. Before dismissing these hypotheses as "just theory," bear with me. Researchers develop theories to make sense of our world, to help us organize our thinking about how things should work and why they should work that way. As it turns out, all of us naturally create implicit theories to help us organize the more immediate world around us. When we see a colleague lash out at someone, we may say, "Wow, they're having a really bad day," or, "Wow, they're an incredible jerk." We don't know for sure why the colleague lashed out—the reason could be some terrible combination of a jerk having a bad day—but we develop our personal theory about why they acted that way.

We also develop theories so we can plan for the next situation. If we conclude that our angry colleague is a good person having a bad day, we might cut them a little slack or wait until tomorrow to ask them a challenging question (or put off a terrible performance review centered on their interactions with colleagues). If we conclude that this colleague is a jerk, we may avoid them altogether.

Theories help us understand our world and recognize how we should act in future situations. In the case of stress, theories can help us understand why we are so stressed out, how we react to stressors, and why some people seem to deal with stress with ease while others experience burnout in response to their stress.

The Transaction Stress Theory

One of the more influential theories about stress was proposed in the mid-1980s by Richard Lazarus and Susan Folkman. Their theory—the transaction stress theory—is based on an individual's appraisal of their environment. When faced with something potentially stressful, individuals make two appraisals of their situation. In the *primary appraisal,* they determine whether they have a stake in what is happening to them and whether it might hinder their personal goals (Lazarus and Folkman 1984). In other words, they try to determine whether they are facing a stressor. For example, when a new patient is admitted to the intensive care unit (ICU), the staff face an additional demand. However, they may or may not perceive this demand as stress-inducing. If the unit is unusually busy that day and no bed is available, the new patient will likely be seen as a significant stressor. On the other hand, if relatively little is happening on the unit at the time, the new patient may be seen as a welcome break from boredom. A situation can be either stressful or a minor blip on the radar, depending on such contextual factors as what else we are doing at the moment, the other demands we are facing, and who is around to help us.

If, in the first appraisal, a person determines that a stressor does exist (e.g., that extra patient is going to be a stressor), they make a *secondary appraisal:* They consider whether they possess the personal resources to cope with the stressor. Depending on the outcome of this evaluation, an individual will determine how best to cope. This determination is what enables some people to handle a stressful situation with relative ease. If members of that ICU staff are accustomed to busy days, bed shortages, and challenging patients, they may have structures in place that allow them to easily deal with the situation.

Lazarus and Folkman (1984) proposed that we cope with our stressors in a variety of ways. Two of these ways are active coping and avoidant coping. *Active coping* refers to the use of methods to manage a situation to regain control; *avoidant coping* refers to avoidance of the situations that cause stress. People are more likely to use active coping when their secondary appraisal suggests that they have the ability and resources to make changes that will improve the stressful situation. On the other hand, when people perceive that the situation cannot be changed or that they do not have the resources to initiate a change, they are more likely to use avoidant coping. You might think of this distinction in terms of "fight or flight." If we have the resources to fight, we do. If we don't have those resources, we run.

While the transaction stress theory has been useful for decades and is well supported by evidence, it still leaves us with some questions. The theory proposes that we assess whether we have the resources to deal with a situation, but it does not define resources or explain how we use our resources. To help address some of the questions left unanswered by the transaction stress theory, we turn to another stress theory that has attracted the attention of many researchers in healthcare (see Prapanjaroensin, Patrican, and Vance 2017): the conservation of resources theory.

Conservation of Resources Theory

Proposed by Stevan Hobfoll several years after the transaction stress theory, the conservation of resources theory emphasizes the role of motivational resources, defined as objects, states, personal characteristics, and symbols that we value because they help us to attain our goals and can be expended to gain additional resources. Hobfoll (1988) developed a list of common resources, which include a home (object), employment (state), self-esteem (personal characteristics), and money (symbols). Conservation of resources theory argues that the key is to understand our "resource account" from which we might draw and how we use those resources.

According to the theory, our stress results from one of three triggers. The first is a loss of resources. Loss of employment, for example, is a significant stressor for most people. This example is rather dramatic; there are other less significant resource losses that we experience. For example, when someone shows up late for an appointment, we have lost time waiting. A public reprimand may cause us to lose self-efficacy and status. Resignation of a close colleague may mean we have lost a valued relationship. The point is the same: If we draw on our pool of resources against our will, we experience stress.

The second trigger is the perception that our resources are threatened. While the COVID-19 pandemic presented healthcare professionals with very real concerns, the lingering uncertainty about the course of the pandemic and how it would affect each individual healthcare professional led to additional stress merely through the perceived threat that the pandemic would likely have additional negative impact at some point.

The third trigger is situations in which the resource investments we have made are not producing gains. To acquire and protect resources, we typically need to invest them in other areas. For example, training to become a healthcare professional requires an investment of time, money, and energy. However, that investment yields skills and employment opportunities (many, in fact, given shortages in most healthcare professions). Once that training is completed, further investment of time and energy will be required for it to yield resources, such as money and job satisfaction. As we acquire resources, we put them to work to gain new and better resources. Sometimes, however, those investments don't work out as we had hoped, and the result is stress. If you spent years attaining a master's degree in health administration with the hopes of getting a promotion and it did not happen, you would likely experience stress.

This last trigger is crucial to our discussion of stress and strain at work. Later in this chapter, I will review some of the most common stressors faced by healthcare professionals (both clinical and administrative staff). Most of these stressors involve an inadequate return on resource investments. People invest a lot to become healthcare professionals and to do their jobs. While many think of healthcare jobs as noble professions, much of the work done in healthcare goes unrecognized. For many, it is a thankless job.

The resource investment process is also important because we use it to deal with the first two stress triggers (loss of resources and threat of loss). When we face resource loss (or threat of loss), we typically invest additional resources to minimize the loss. When we think we might lose our job, we invest time to update our resume, search for job openings, and tap our network for job opportunities. Thus, according to the conservation of resources theory, coping is an investment of resources. When we have a lot of resources, we engage in more active coping. When we don't have resources, we lean toward avoidant coping.

Conservation of Resources Theory

According to conservation of resources theory, our stress comes from three sources (with examples):

- Loss of resources, such as:
    - Job loss
    - Resignation of a close coworker

- Threat to resources, such as:
    - Media reports about job losses
    - Proposed changes to reimbursement

- Bad investment of resources, such as:
    - Working on a project but not receiving recognition for doing so
    - Helping a friend (or patient) but not receiving a reciprocal favor
    - Achieving a degree but not finding a job or getting a promotion

Understanding resource investment helps us understand how we go from experiencing stress to burning out. Recall from the introduction that burnout is a response to extreme work stress. It is the point where we can't take any more stress, where we are exhausted. According to the conservation of resources theory, we reach a point where we keep investing resources to cope with stressors but don't get anything back to replenish the resources that we use. Eventually, we run out of resources; our account is empty. As we'll discuss later in this chapter, arrival at this juncture leads to a whole host of problems, including burnout.

How We Will Use These Theories

So why have I spent so much page space on stress theories? Why don't I get to the meat of the issue and talk about what is causing stress in healthcare? The theories help us understand the stressors and why they are stressful, which in turn will hopefully help us design system-level changes to address them. The reality is, though, that healthcare professionals will still experience stress. Fifty years ago, healthcare providers experienced stress. They may not have been dealing with complex issues of coordination of care, pay for performance, and advanced technologies, but they experienced stress, nonetheless. Even a decade ago when I wrote the first edition of this book, I would have never anticipated the extent to which a global pandemic would lead to the stress and burnout of healthcare professionals. Fifty years from now, we may have solved many of the problems I will describe in the next paragraphs, but new concerns will likely emerge. When they do, healthcare professionals will deal with them by using the same processes. They will assess whether the concerns are stressors, evaluate whether their resources match the demands placed on them, and invest some of those resources to deal with the stressors. An understanding of the specific stressors people face may be useful to have, but more important is the process they follow to deal with those stressors. While our context (and thus our stressors) will change, the psychological processes we use to cope with those stressors likely will not.

The theories are also useful because they give us direction for dealing with the stressors. If we know that stress results from issues with our resources, replacing those resources and building new resources probably will help to alleviate it. Later in the book, I will discuss the development of such solutions. For the moment, let's consider some of the common stressors that healthcare professionals face.

STRESSORS AMONG CLINICAL STAFF

All clinical staffs regularly face a common list of stressors. While a complete list of these stressors is beyond the scope of this book (and could take up several volumes), a number of key stressors are worthy of exploration, either because I have encountered them frequently in my discussions with healthcare professionals, because they are frequently discussed in the literature, or because they are much worse (or much less worse) than people realize.

Patient Demands

Perhaps the most obvious stressor faced by healthcare professionals is the demand placed on them by patients. The daily grind of meeting with patients, explaining diagnoses, devising and implementing treatment plans, and answering their questions requires considerable investment of resources. Remember, however, that healthcare professionals are trained to deal with these types of demands and usually are able to deal with even particularly difficult cases and patients. Often, the stressors in the broader organizational context that were not addressed in their training or for which their training doesn't quite align to their current situation cause the most stress. For example, even if there was some coverage of electronic health record use in their training, the significant variations and seemingly endless changes to the user interfaces are a significant source of stress for healthcare providers.

By suggesting these types of stressors are the more persistent stressors in healthcare, I am not diminishing the emotional stress associated with caring for patients. In recent years, the term "compassion fatigue" has become common in research and popular press, particularly in light of the challenges faced by healthcare providers during the COVID-19 pandemic. While there is little doubt that working with patients takes an emotional toll on healthcare professionals, several authors have raised concerns about how compassion fatigue is being conceptualized.

University of Calgary researcher Shane Sinclair has been researching the topic of compassion in healthcare for many years. His team carefully analyzed 91 studies of the topic and concluded that compassion fatigue has been ill-defined and inappropriately measured by researchers. A very brief search of the research on this topic will quickly reveal confusion. Is compassion fatigue an acute reaction to situations or chronic issue, and does it contribute to burnout? Or is burnout actually a component of compassion fatigue? As a result, the inordinate attention being paid to the topic may be masking other important issues of well-being and other stressors in healthcare workplaces (Sinclair et al. 2017).

To be clear, working with patients certainly affects healthcare professionals, and compassion fatigue—while ill-defined—remains a stressor to be mindful of. However, when it comes to interventions, and especially with our limited available time and resources, there is typically greater value in focusing on areas where we can make changes. In the end, stress from working with patients will always be there. The vast majority of healthcare professionals know, or learn very quickly in their training, that compassion fatigue will occur. While there may be some benefit to learning better coping mechanisms, paying greater attention to aspects of the work environment we have control over will be more effective over the long term.

Workload, Staffing, and Scheduling

Issues of workload, staffing, and scheduling are significant, interrelated sources of stress for many healthcare professionals. In a systematic review of 91 studies of nursing burnout, Dall'Ora and colleagues (2020) found that high workload, inadequate staffing levels, and great time pressure were among the most common stressors for nurses. As a result of low staffing levels, professionals are more likely to work less-desirable schedules and have a greater overall workload. Even in studies conducted during the height of the COVID-19 pandemic, workload and insufficient staffing were identified as common stressors, alongside the more obvious stress of the threat of contracting COVID-19 (Galanis et al. 2021). These issues are not necessarily quickly resolved: As I have noted, even if organizations had the resources (time and money) to address staffing issues, the pool of qualified healthcare professionals seeking employment may not be large enough to meet their needs.

With regard to scheduling, the most stressful issues appear to be working overnight shifts, long shifts (longer than 12 hours), and mandatory overtime. The common theme is interference with other aspects of life. Working overnight shifts makes other social aspects of life difficult, and working mandatory overtime makes balancing work and nonwork life challenging because of a lack of predictability.

Working with Other Professionals

We all know that dealing with other people can cause stress. In the review by Dall'Ora and colleagues (2020) mentioned earlier, a negative nurse–physician relationship, negative team relationship, and poor leadership were all identified as common causes of burnout. The high degrees of autonomy and professionalism in healthcare, as well as historical hierarchical structures, have made communication among healthcare professionals challenging.

Some of the concern about working with other professionals goes back to matters of leadership. A large-scale study found that a 1-point improvement in leadership (as rated in a survey) yielded a 7 percent decrease in burnout in the sample of nonphysician healthcare employees (Dyrbye et al. 2020). In another review of the literature, this time focused on leadership styles, Wei and colleagues (2020) found that the transactional leadership style, which concentrates on intervention as a means of correcting behavior (called *management by exception*), is more likely perceived as a stressor by staff. This outcome may result from how frontline managers are typically chosen in healthcare—that is, for their expertise (e.g., they are great nurses, physicians, or technicians) and not their leadership skills. These managers typically draw from technical expertise to look for deviations from accepted practice rather than proactively address the work environment to make it better.

So, what does work? Research, including the studies mentioned here, finds that authentic leadership and strong individualized relationships with employees that emphasize psychological safety are helpful in reducing burnout (Kelly and Hearld 2020; Ma et al. 2021). I will elaborate on how you can put these ideas into action later in the book.

Working with Technology

As a result of the quality movement in healthcare, greater emphasis has been placed on using technology to improve outcomes. However, research suggests that these technologies are frequently implemented without fully considering their impact on the employees using them. Technology that is intended to make jobs easier becomes a significant stressor for healthcare professionals because of the learning curve involved in navigating a new system. Indeed, many professionals find ways of working around the technology to avoid the stress it causes them. In some cases, the work-around bypasses the safety gains that the technology was meant to provide.

The stress associated with implementation of new technologies often reveals a broader stressor among clinical staff: poorly designed work process. Blocks in the process resulting from poor process or system design are a significant source of frustration for healthcare professionals. In my research, when I have asked physicians, nurses, pharmacists, and other healthcare professionals about how they feel when they have to alter their work processes in response to poor work design, the near-universal answer is "frustrated." That they come up with their own solutions for how the work should be done highlights an issue from the introduction that we will elaborate on later in the book: They know how to fix the problem. They have the solutions and are ready to implement them. However, if we don't capture their ideas in a systematic way, we end up with idiosyncratic solutions to the problem that make healthcare processes unreliable.

STRESSORS FOR ADMINISTRATIVE STAFF

In some ways, the stressors described in the previous paragraphs are also stressors for administrators. Stressors experienced by clinical staff will likely make their way upstream and become problems that administrators are left to address—and poor leadership is a stressor for administrative staff just as it is for clinical staff.

Moreover, the stressors discussed earlier have other implications for administrators. For example, staffing shortages affect administrators who must fill open positions and retain the staff they have. They must also schedule work in ways that optimize resources. Clearly, these circumstances can lead to stress. Administrators have stressors of their own to contend with, as well.

Coordination of the Clinical Function

Much of the coordination of the clinical function falls on administrators, and it is a stressful aspect of their job. Managing the intricacies of professional autonomy, personality differences, and different resource needs is a tremendous challenge.

In addition to actual coordination of the clinical function, administrators are charged with making patients' care *appear* coordinated. In other words, care that is coordinated in a computer system or among the clinical staff may appear disjointed to the patient. Think of the times you have gone to the doctor and received a bill with six or seven different charges, when you thought you had undergone only a single simple procedure. The management of public perception is a notable stressor for many administrators.

The Quality Movement

Reports from the Institute of Medicine over the past few decades have put tremendous pressure on administrators to shore up the quality of the healthcare provided in their facilities. This charge has subjected administrators to the challenges of measuring and reporting quality indicators, meeting the needs of regulatory and accrediting bodies, and shifting the culture of the organization to a sharper focus on quality. Cultural change is one of the most difficult things for a leader to initiate. People are inherently risk-averse and change-avoidant; healthcare professionals are arguably even more risk-averse than average and typically demand evidence before they agree to support change initiatives.

The quality movement is also subjecting administrators to financial stress. As payers increasingly hold healthcare organizations accountable for medical errors by not reimbursing for them, administrators are applying pressure to minimize their occurrence. As discussed in chapter 1, their job is made more difficult because stress among clinical staff may reduce the likelihood that they will report near-miss information that would be helpful in error prevention.

Issues of coordination and quality can also intersect to create entirely new stressors. I've frequently observed this phenomenon in the context of quality improvement training. To improve patient safety through better teamwork, many organizations have implemented crew resource management training programs. Ideally, these programs concurrently train clinical teams that work together so they can easily transfer what they have learned into practice. This design is rarely practical, however. For one thing, shutting down a unit so everyone can attend training may not be feasible. Further, physicians often will not commit to full-day training sessions of this nature. As a result, they may separately attend a shorter version of the training program that is not conducted at the same time as their colleagues' program. In another example, I've observed resident physicians trained in teamwork and communication skills defer to the methods of attending physicians who had not received the same training.

The stressors discussed here do not form an exhaustive list, but rather only a sampling of the sources of stress healthcare professionals face. After stressors have been identified, the next challenge is to understand how individuals cope with those stressors, as their coping patterns play a key role in whether that stress becomes burnout.

COPING WITH STRESS

Research evidence has been clear regarding the consequences of using active or avoidant coping. Benefits (in terms of future psychological symptoms) consistently follow the use of active coping, while negative consequences result from reliance on avoidance strategies. That is not to say that avoidant coping doesn't play a role in dealing with stress. Sometimes, taking time to avoid the stressor may keep someone from acting in a rash manner and making the situation worse (e.g., lashing out at the boss over a minor stressor). Remember, however, that avoiding the stressor doesn't make it go away. It will be there when you come back to it. This inevitable outcome is part of the reason intervention strategies based on avoidance, discussed in more detail in chapters 5 and 6, don't work. You can take a one-week vacation to "get away from it all," but when you leave the beach, that crummy job will still be waiting—with a week's worth of piled-up work!

Coping is a key link in the progression from stress to burnout. People who cope well with their stressors do not experience burnout. Those who don't cope well are more likely to reach that stage.

Coping with Stress

While there are many ways to cope with stress, the most common distinction is between:

- Active coping—methods that are used to manage a situation so as to regain control, such as:
    - Talking with your supervisor
    - Developing an action plan for addressing workload
    - Proposing changes to work process

- Avoidant coping—avoidance of the situations that cause stress, such as:
    - Avoiding troublesome staff on the unit
    - Missing meetings in which difficult topics are likely to come up
    - Delegating decisions you should be making yourself

WHEN STRESS BECOMES BURNOUT

Burnout is a response to chronic work stress. While the manifestation of burnout has been the subject of considerable scholarly debate, this chapter emphasizes the most common perceptions of the burnout experience. The following discussion builds on the traditional three-component conceptualization of burnout that dates back to the early 1980s and the work of Christina Maslach (1982). Her work focused on emotional exhaustion, disengagement, and reduced personal efficacy.

Exhaustion

Exhaustion is the feeling that you have depleted your resources. When people say they are emotionally drained or they don't have any more to give, they are experiencing exhaustion. One of my favorite ways to assess exhaustion is to ask the respondent to indicate the extent to which the following statement applies: "When I wake up in the morning, I already feel too tired to go to work." I think the feeling described in that statement is the essence of exhaustion, and burnout in general. The mere thought of work is tiring.

Exhaustion is typically considered the core of the burnout experience. This designation is based on two ideas. First, despite considerable scholarly debate, all notable conceptualizations of burnout include some aspect of exhaustion. Second, research suggests that this symptom of burnout tends to appear first and leads to the other two symptoms. Therefore, to understand the burnout experience, first understand the nature of exhaustion.

While early conceptualizations of exhaustion were centered on emotional exhaustion, they have since been expanded to include cognitive and physical exhaustion. In other words, an employee can be "fed up" with work (emotionally exhausted), not have the cognitive resources to think straight, or be physically worn out by the job.

Disengagement

Disengagement occurs when a healthcare professional starts to pull away from work.

Disengagement is a way of coping with the excessive stress that led to exhaustion. People naturally pull away from jobs that wear them out. They have two choices in that situation: fight or flight. If employees have reached the point of exhaustion, however, they will realize that attempts at fighting are likely to be ineffective. Instead, they will try to distance themselves from the sources of stress. Poor treatment of others, reduced voluntary activity at work, absenteeism, and even turnover are all manifestations of disengagement.

Reduced Professional Efficacy

Employees experiencing the third symptom of burnout, reduced professional efficacy, believe their ability to perform their job has diminished. On the surface, this symptom seems like a natural reaction to the first two symptoms. If a job is wearing an employee out and they are pulling away from it, they might feel as though they are not as good at the job as they once were.

As part of the burnout concept, this symptom is somewhat controversial. Although reduced efficacy was a part of Maslach's original conceptualization, most contemporary researchers no longer consider it a symptom of burnout. It's not that people react to stress differently than they once did; rather, recent empirical research has found that professional efficacy is more likely either a consequence of emotional exhaustion and disengagement or a parallel development. Professional efficacy is related to burnout, but not a confirmed component of burnout. For this reason, the rest of the book will focus on exhaustion and disengagement. Nevertheless, efficacy does play a role in the process and is a key element of job performance. Because people must feel capable of performance to be able to perform, efficacy is an important variable to consider.

THE BREAKING POINT

At what point does stress become burnout? The turning point between the two is not known. Quite a few researchers have used arbitrary points on burnout or stress scales (covered in chapter 4) to determine whether someone is burned out. For example, if someone scores an average of 4 out of 5 on a burnout scale, that person might be considered burned out. This approach is useful in that statements like "X percent of our workforce is burned out" can be drawn; however, it assumes that everyone responds the same way to survey questions, and a multitude of evidence suggests that this is not the case.

Instead of trying to identify the turning point, a better objective might be to decide whether we need to pinpoint one at all. The terms *stress* and *strain* (which burnout represents) are engineering terms; a bridge experiences stress each time a car goes over it and experiences strain when it starts to crack. We don't wait until the bridge collapses to say it is strained. Moreover, there may be differences in the severity of strain. As a result, most researchers treat burnout as a variable rather than designate a point at which burnout occurs. Burnout is commonly referred to in a discrete sense ("I'm burned out"), but degrees are often added to it as well ("I'm *really* burned out"). In this book, burnout will be treated as a continuum, although discrete phrasing may be used in some cases for purposes of simplicity.

Everyone experiences stress, but why doesn't everyone experience burnout? A variety of factors might help explain why some people reach the breaking point of burnout and others do not.

WHAT DOESN'T CAUSE STRESS AND BURNOUT?

That heading is perhaps a bit misleading. There certainly are all kinds of things that have no relationship with stress and burnout. In this section, we'll look at variables that are not as closely linked to stress and burnout as people might think. For example, some studies attest that there is a relationship between gender and burnout, while others claim there is no association between the two. This discrepancy brings up two important issues. The first is causality. Gender does not *cause* burnout; one is not destined to be burned out because of one's gender. Instead, gender often co-varies with other causes of burnout, such as work–family expectations, workload, and other gender-role factors.

The second issue is data consistency. While more studies seem to show that burnout rates are higher among women, plenty of studies show that men have higher burnout rates. This finding may also be linked to the occupations of the participants in the study. For many years, the emphasis in the burnout literature was on service sectors (especially nursing and teaching) that tended to employ more women than men. Workers in these sectors also tend to experience higher burnout rates because their jobs involve working with people. The bottom line is that gender is likely not associated with burnout at all, or if it is, it is a meager, spurious association that could be better explained by examining specific dynamics of work, such as workload.

A similar explanation exists for studies that have found relationships between age and organizational tenure. Those variables are already highly related to each other (as we stick around our organizations, we get older) and appear to be negatively associated with burnout. In other words, people with longer tenure seem to experience lower burnout. But does our burnout really diminish over time? As we get used to the way things work, our stress may abate. As we gain experience, we may be assigned better projects. In both cases, the relationship between age/tenure and burnout is better explained by some other factor such as maturation or work assignments and not by age or tenure, per se. Retention is also important. People who are highly burned out are more likely to leave their jobs—the ultimate form of disengagement. Thus, those who stay around and have longer tenure likely experience less burnout.

The intent of the past two paragraphs is not to critique the research but to draw attention to a trap that managers occasionally fall into when drawing such conclusions as, "Women are more burned out; I should develop a program for them," or "I need to target the young people." Those statements might be true, but not because they are women or young, but rather because of other factors. Perhaps they aren't getting the support they need, their expectations of the job are not being fulfilled, or some other factor is affecting their work. When we develop interventions, we need to figure out what we can change, and gender and age are two things we obviously cannot change.

HOW STABLE IS BURNOUT?

If someone reports high burnout today, is that person likely to report high burnout again six months or a year from now? Empirical studies of burnout tend to find high correlations over time, but we must be careful not to equate correlations over time with stability of the burnout experience. Correlations are drawn from a pattern of scores across individuals in a sample. If one person's burnout score is higher today than it was yesterday and others in the study follow the same pattern, a strong positive correlation would be made. Does the presence of a correlation mean their scores are stable? No. It means their burnout has increased over time in a manner consistent with the others that were measured, so that their rank order of burnout scores remains largely the same. (Burnout scores are discussed further in chapter 4.)

That said, there are ways to assess stability over time by making statistical corrections to the correlations. In doing so, studies have found relatively high consistency over time. They also have found that, in general, the time frame of the study is irrelevant. Studies that have explored consistency over time frames of three months to five years have obtained similar results.

These findings suggest that the factors underlying burnout are consistent over time. If you have a poor leader today and the same poor leader is in place a year from now, why would you expect burnout to change? The findings also support the idea that avoidant coping is not effective in dealing with stress. If the underlying causes of burnout are stable, avoiding the stressors isn't going to make them go away.

TAKEAWAY POINTS: TO MANAGE STRESS AND AVOID BURNOUT, FIRST UNDERSTAND THE ROLE OF RESOURCES

In this chapter, we covered the main theories about stress management as well as some of the primary stressors facing clinicians and administrators that can lead to burnout. The goal was to give you a framework for thinking about stress and burnout. The logic presented in this chapter suggests that if we manage our staffs' resources by providing what they need to face their everyday demands at work, we can significantly reduce the stress they face and, hopefully, reduce the likelihood that they experience burnout.

The following list includes key points covered in this chapter:

- Stress results when the demands of our job exceed the resources we possess to deal with those demands.
- When we face a potential stressor, we cognitively evaluate whether we are actually facing a stressor and whether we can deal with it.
- Our stressors come from three primary processes: (1) loss of our resources, (2) threats to our resources, and (3) bad investment of our resources.
- Common stressors among clinical staff include patient demands, workload, scheduling, working with others, and working with technology. Common stressors among administrative staff (in addition to those just listed) include coordination and quality.

- Chronic stress leads to burnout, which is characterized by exhaustion, disengagement, and, in some cases, reduced personal efficacy.
- Everyone experiences stress, but not everyone experiences burnout, so studies on burnout are primarily concerned with what causes stress to progress to burnout. Personal and organizational factors can influence the connection between stress and burnout.

FURTHER READING

Dall'Ora, C., J. Ball, M. Reinius, and P. Griffiths. 2020. "Burnout in Nursing: A Theoretical Review." *Human Resources for Health* 18 (1): 1–17. https://doi.org/10.1186/s12960-020-00469-9.

National Academies of Sciences, Engineering, and Medicine. 2019. *Taking Action Against Clinician Burnout: A Systems Approach to Professional Well-Being.* Washington, DC: National Academies Press. https://doi.org/10.17226/25521.

CHAPTER 3

Building Employee Engagement

I'm not going to lie. The past year has been rough. Despite everything, I enjoy my work and wouldn't think of doing anything else. I know what we are trying to accomplish and what I need to do to help us achieve those goals. I pour myself into my work because I know it's making a difference.

—Nurse working in rural hospital

I like that when I go to work, I look up at the clock and don't realize that the day has passed me by.

—Urologist working in a community hospital

IN THE YEARS since writing the first edition of this book, the interest in the concept of employee engagement has really been embraced by researchers, the popular press, and influential bodies such as the Malcolm Baldrige National Quality Program. A quick search on Google Scholar using "employee engagement healthcare" yielded 15,900 results for the years 2000 through 2009, the ten years leading to the publication of the first edition of this book. For the next ten-year period, the search yielded 53,800 results—a nearly fourfold increase. That interest has continued to explode. In just the first two years of the 2020s, the search yielded a remarkable 42,200 entries. That pace suggests exponential growth in this topic, largely as people have understood the important role that employee engagement plays in so many factors that make organizations successful. In fact, that impact may be even more important in healthcare now than ever before, as the performance of healthcare professionals increasingly serves as a differentiating factor in terms of quality of care, patient safety, and overall organizational performance.

Unfortunately, engagement has not been clearly defined. It means different things depending on whom you ask. In some ways, it becomes a bit more difficult to sort out the actual impact of engagement on organizations if we aren't even sure we are all talking about the same thing.

In this chapter, we will address those different conceptualizations of engagement to help develop consensus about what it means for your employees and your organization. We will review why engagement has become so important by exploring its relationships with important outcomes for healthcare organizations. Finally, we'll begin to examine the underlying factors that lead employees to be more engaged with their organization and with their work.

WHAT IS ENGAGEMENT?

A consistent definition of engagement has been elusive for quite a while. In their book about building engagement to improve employee performance, MacLeod and Clarke (2009) identified 50 definitions of engagement. Saks and Gruman (2014) also pointed out the lack of a common term for the concept, with people using terms such as *personal engagement, employee engagement, job engagement,* and *work engagement.* Different sources will use different terms to mean the same thing or use the same term but define it very differently. A more recent systematic review of the engagement literature found six conceptualizations, or broader ways of thinking about, engagement (Bailey et al. 2017). Though valuable from a research perspective, the distinctions between the conceptualizations and definitions tend to be a bit too narrow to worry about in practice. Instead, I've synthesized those six conceptualizations into two broad notions of engagement: engagement as a state of well-being and engagement as practice. I will review each in this chapter to help you develop more engagement among employees.

Engagement as a State of Well-Being

Most engagement scholars cite a seminal paper by William Kahn (1990) as the starting point for understanding the concept of engagement. He defined *engagement* as "the harnessing of organization members' (preferred) selves to their work roles" (p. 694) and suggested that it can have cognitive, emotional, and physical components. The work that follows Kahn's has generally looked at engagement as a psychological state of being. It may occasionally be measured in behavioral terms, but it's more about how the employee is thinking about their work.

In the years since Kahn's work, researchers have taken his notion of personal engagement with work in a number of unique directions. As with many other psychological concepts, none of these variations is inherently correct or incorrect. Rather, they look at the same concept from slightly different angles.

Dutch researcher Wilmar Schaufeli and colleagues (2002) provide one of the most popular variations of personal engagement. They define engagement in terms of three qualities:

- *Vigor*—the energy that one brings to the job. Engaged individuals bring a lot of energy to their work.
- *Dedication*—the commitment aspect of engagement. Dedicated employees are interested in advancing the organization's mission.
- *Absorption*—a state in which an individual is engrossed in work. Sometimes called "flow," this quality is frequently manifested as losing track of time as a result of being immersed in a task.

Schaufeli and colleagues developed the Utrecht Work Engagement Scale (to be detailed in chapter 4) that assesses each of these three qualities, or components, of engagement. Their conceptualization of engagement is similar to Kahn's initial ideas with its emphasis on individual employees and their relationship with their work. It differs from Kahn's work in that it divides engagement into three components (in part to contrast engagement with the dominant three-facet definition of burnout at the time). Initially, it was believed that the Utrecht team's interest was also in a more general state of engagement, whereas Kahn was thinking about engagement as a momentary, fleeting experience. That may be true of dedication, but vigor and absorption could reasonably be expected to vary quite a bit within a day, depending on the situation the employee is in.

While the Schaufeli/Utrecht approach to engagement is by far the most common in the research literature, others may be more useful if you are observing issues specific to your workplace and hoping to address them. Reflecting Kahn's perspective, several researchers have envisioned engagement in terms of its cognitive, emotional, and physical expression (see Saks 2006; Shirom 2008; Soane et al. 2012; Winton, Cornelius, and Grawitch 2022). In practice, these approaches are not all that different, as one could argue that there are conceptual overlaps between vigor, dedication, and absorption and cognitive, emotional, and physical expression. They share the same theme of considering engagement a multidimensional idea.

The approach to engagement in all of these cases is useful because it helps us think about the various psychological processes that make up engagement. These approaches home in on certain elements of engagement that are relevant to your needs while discarding other elements that are less important to the types of jobs you want to improve.

Engagement as Practice

The other broad way of conceptualizing engagement looks at engagement as something that employees do. That is, it is based on a set of specific behaviors that can be managed rather than a state of being. Proponents of this approach emphasize not only the behaviors of the engaged employee but also the behaviors of others (e.g., supervisors) that help set up the conditions for success at work. This management-centric idea of engagement as practice emanated from the work of researchers in human resource management and major consulting firms such as Gallup rather than from work of psychologists and organizational behavior scholars such as Kahn and Schaufeli.

While measures of engagement are described in chapter 4, understanding this perspective might be easiest by noting at this point how engagement is assessed in this conceptualization. Measures will frequently take into account the presence or lack of feedback at work, friends at work, clear expectations about performance, involvement at work, and professional development. Job satisfaction and commitment to the organization may also be measured.

On the one hand, this approach can be very appealing. By emphasizing the behaviors of engaged employees and the conditions that led to that engagement, it can translate well into actions to workplace improvements. On the other hand, this approach also assumes that those conditions lead to engagement. They often do, but not always. An employee may receive information about expectations at work but find that they change frequently and without warning. Feedback may even conflict with those expectations. I want to emphasize that it is better to have performance feedback, clear expectations, opportunities to grow, and similar conditions than it is to not have these features as part of one's job. We just don't know if they necessarily lead someone to be engaged.

Which Approach to Engagement Is Better?

So, which approach is the way to go? Is it better to focus on engagement as a state of being or as a practice?

Neither is really better than the other. Yes, this response from an academic may elicit an eye-roll, but in this case, the approaches are not really in competition. They just describe different things. Reflect on a time when you felt really "into" your work. If I asked you to describe that time, you might talk about how you were really excited, laser-focused, and fully satisfied with the situation. Or you might tell me about the project you were working on, who else was involved, and the tasks at hand during that time. Both answers are legitimate descriptions of your engagement with work. Neither is wrong; they are just different.

Even proponents of each approach recognize the value of the other perspective. For example, researchers who look at the psychology of engagement may also look at the resources that are most likely to lead to a psychological state of engagement—and the resources they measure sound a lot like the conditions for engagement from the engagement as practice approach. For example, in a very large study of employees at IBM, Cooper-Thomas and colleagues (2018) measured resources such as learning and development opportunities and belief in the vision of the organization to determine which were most associated with higher engagement.

From a practical standpoint, those varying conceptualizations are rather useful. The psychological approach is most helpful if you are trying to capture whether and to what extent your employees are engaged with their work. It would be useful in evaluating an intervention to see if there were meaningful changes in engagement. On the other hand, the management practice–focused approach may be more useful as you develop ideas for interventions. Because they typically measure the conditions that lead to engagement or behaviors that are indicative of engagement, interventions in those areas may be logical starting points for interventions. Depending on the approach you take, using measurements that are aligned with this perspective could give you an early indicator of whether an intervention is working.

Returning to the question at the start of this section, engagement can mean many different things. Most succinctly, however, it is feeling a very strong connection between one's work and oneself in a way that motivates each of us to do great things. Whether that comes in the form of attitudes, behaviors, or both, it is something we hope to achieve in all of our employees.

THE VALUE OF ENGAGEMENT

Organizations want employees to be engaged. In some ways, that's a bit obvious—one can imagine little value in a workforce that is not engaged. But the value of engagement is also backed by the evidence. Research has found that engaged employees perform at higher levels and are less likely to leave the organization (Neuber et al. 2022). As the first quotation opening the chapter suggests, engaged employees wake up in the morning and *want* to go to work. Healthcare organizations want to employ these kinds of people, not only because they will be highly productive but also because they will truly satisfy the patients with whom they interact. They will take the time necessary to ensure that each patient receives the highest quality of care possible. They will be sure to follow patient safety procedures because they recognize their importance.

Let's take a closer look at the evidence to support these ideas. There is a lot of overlap between the outcomes of burnout and engagement, with burnout associated with the negative experience of those outcomes (e.g., lower performance) and engagement associated with the positive experience (e.g., better performance). I'll briefly address those outcomes but give a little more space to emphasizing unique advantages of engagement as it relates to burnout.

Performance, Quality of Care, and Patient Safety

Just as burnout leads to lower performance and concerns about patient safety, engagement leads to higher performance and safer practices by healthcare professionals. For example, a systematic review by Keyko and colleagues (2016) found consistent positive effects of engagement on nurse performance. A large meta-analysis of studies (combining multiple quantitative research studies) by Wee and Lai (2022) found fairly consistent relationships between engagement and clinicians' self-ratings of patient care quality. Prins and colleagues (2009) examined data from 2,115 resident physicians in the Netherlands and found that highly engaged physicians were less likely to make mistakes.

Engagement also affects performance and practice when analyzed at the organizational level. Perhaps one of the most comprehensive examinations of these outcomes was published by West and Dawson (2012) using data from the UK National Health Service (NHS) Staff Survey. Their analysis is noteworthy for two reasons: (1) it included more than 150,000 staff from almost 400 healthcare organizations within the NHS, and (2) they were able to connect the data from each healthcare organization with independent data on key performance and safety outcomes.

What they found is consistent with what you would expect. Organizations with higher levels of engagement had higher levels of patient satisfaction, quality of services, and financial performance. They also found that organizations with higher engagement had lower levels of absenteeism, turnover, and patient mortality (even after accounting for previous patient mortality rates, in order to identify the role engagement would play). Their findings have been replicated by RAND Europe (Hafner et al. 2020) and Wake and Green (2019) using more recent NHS data.

Unique Benefits of Engagement

In addition to the expected outcomes of engagement, researchers have discovered other outcomes that add to the value of developing an engaged workforce. I will note that the research on these topics is still emerging, so some of what I'll share has not necessarily been tested in healthcare settings. Nonetheless, just as nearly all the findings shared in this book have been consistent in both healthcare and non-healthcare settings, we would expect that, with time, these findings will be confirmed among healthcare professionals.

An emerging line of research is finding that engagement facilitates creativity and innovation in organizations (see Kwon and Kim 2020 for a review of these studies). Specifically, engaged employees appear to exhibit more innovative behavior (coming up with new ideas for challenges at work) and are more willing to share knowledge with others in the workplace. Given the important role that problem-solving plays in healthcare settings, both for clinical and administrative staff, this is a very positive outcome to consider. Note that high levels of resources tend to lead to virtuous cycles of engagement and positive outcomes, suggesting that engagement leads to innovation and success with those innovative behaviors enhances engagement (Gawke, Gorgievski, and Bakker 2017).

Too Much of a Good Thing?

Before turning to the conditions that facilitate engagement among healthcare professionals, I want to issue a word of caution: It is possible for employees to be too engaged. For example, in earlier work (Halbesleben, Harvey, and Bolino 2009), I noticed that engagement scores in the data we had collected were positively correlated with work–family conflict or feeling like one's job is interfering with family life. As we dug deeper, we found that some of the benefits of engagement—particularly higher levels of performance of organizational citizenship behaviors (going above and beyond what is expected)—were leading to those conflicts.

Before you walk away wondering why you just read through all the previous material if engagement can be a bad thing, let me be clear that there are some important caveats to its negative effects. First, that connection between engagement and work–family conflict is there when the engagement manifests itself in the form of excessive work behavior on the part of the employee. In fact, if you were to measure only engagement and work–family conflict among staff, you might even find that they are negatively correlated with each other (i.e., higher engagement is associated with lower work–family conflict). The key here is whether those high levels of engagement lead to work behaviors that obstruct family relationships.

In our 2009 study that tied engagement to a higher degree of work–family conflict, another very important factor became evident: how conscientious the employee was. Conscientious employees are highly motivated to achieve, but they also are better at managing their time and other resources in ways that facilitate high achievement at work without sacrificing other aspects of their life. Conscientiousness short-circuits the engagement and work–family conflict relationship because conscientious employees have better strategies to avoid letting work overtake family.

The relationship between engagement and creativity also has a potential downside. This might be most clear in the literature on job crafting, which occurs when employees adjust their work to better align their jobs with their goals. This is a manifestation of creativity for many employees as they shape their jobs toward tasks they prefer and are better at, or at least think they are better at. Engaged employees are more active in job crafting, which, in turn, increases their engagement. Frequently, this is a good thing for both the employees and the organization. But as I've written elsewhere (Halbesleben 2021), there can be a cost if it is not managed well. Consider, for example, your highly engaged employee who has managed to craft their job such that it looks nothing like what you thought you were paying them to do. When their engagement is directed toward tasks that add little value to your organization, that's clearly not helpful.

Returning to an issue raised in chapter 1, when job creativity shows up in the form of work-arounds, patient safety becomes a concern. Generally, we would expect engaged employees not to develop work-arounds because they possess the wherewithal to really delve into what's causing the work-around and what needs to be fixed. However, there can be instances where employees apply work-arounds to free up the time they need to engage in aspects of the job they prefer. In those circumstances, we have to direct that engagement to where it needs to be focused. Fortunately, performance feedback is a really good way to increase engagement! With that as our segue, let's explore conditions that help make engagement more likely among employees.

HOW CAN WE FOSTER ENGAGEMENT?

So, what leads employees to become engaged? Theoretically, the processes underlying resources discussed earlier (e.g., resource loss/gains and resource investment) are useful in understanding engagement because those underlying processes both lead to, or reduce, burnout and engagement.

To be clear, simply addressing burnout will not yield engagement. Burnout and engagement follow related, parallel processes, but they are not two ends of the same continuum. A point can be reached at which burnout has been eliminated, but elimination of burnout does not automatically transform into engagement. At the point where burnout no longer exists, you will need to switch over to a parallel, positive process of developing engagement (see exhibit 3.1).

That positive process toward engagement involves ensuring employees have adequate resources to be successful in their work and don't perceive that their resources will be threatened. Of course, those resources won't last forever; most people don't assume just because they have enough slack time to comfortably do their job now that it will always be that way. In engagement, fearing the threat of lost resources is less important than understanding clearly the conditions under which those resources would be reduced. Think of it this way: If you looked at your calendar for next week and saw you had some blocks of free time to start the week, you might take advantage of that opportunity to spend time on bigger-picture initiatives that you really enjoy working on and could make a big difference. You might also see that the end of your week is loaded

Exhibit 3.1 Burnout and Engagement as Parallel Processes

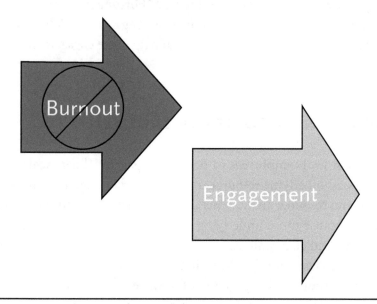

with meetings, which doesn't necessarily reduce your engagement in those big initiatives. The time is still there to tackle them.

A large-scale study of healthcare professionals in Minnesota supported the idea that resources can lead to engagement. Koranne and colleagues (2022) found that resources such as sufficient time, an efficient team, and autonomy and control over work were associated with higher levels of engagement among physicians, advanced practice nurses, and physician assistants. Other studies have found similar findings with nurses (Van Bogaert et al. 2017) and occupational therapists (Poulsen et al. 2014).

Engagement also follows the processes regarding resource investment outlined in conservation of resources theory. Recall that burnout results when resources are invested without adequate return. As Crawford and colleagues (2013) note, a "key driver of engagement is employees' experience of psychological meaningfulness, or the sense of receiving a return on investment of their self in work role performances" (p. 62).

In summary, engagement is developed when employees feel they have adequate resources to invest in their work, understand where those resources are coming from and how their availability fluctuates, and feel that the investment of their resources will pay off in the long run. An interesting illustration of how this process works, and how it is similar but not quite the same as burnout, was illustrated in a meta-analysis by the same team led by Crawford and colleagues (2010). They took a step beyond demands placed on employees' resources by looking at the specific nature of those demands. Specifically, they examined the differences between hindrance demands, which are obstacles in our work that impede us from reaching our goals, and challenge demands, which are short-term demands that we understand are necessary to reach our goals. They found that the demands of both hindrances and challenges lead to higher burnout; they are, after all, demands that expend our resources. They also found that hindrance demands lead to lower engagement, largely because they must be addressed but don't contribute to achieving goals. However, they found that challenge demands lead to higher engagement. This makes sense. Those demands require investment of resources, but they also should lead to a positive outcome as a result of those investments.

So, possessing resources leads to engagement just as lacking them causes stress, which leads to burnout. Sounds simple enough. But if it were truly that simple, why aren't more employees engaged? It turns out burnout is more often caused by a smaller number of more fundamental resource losses or threats than engagement. If we don't have basic resources necessary to do our job, burnout is likely to occur. But having those basic needs in place is unlikely to lead to engagement (though they must be in place to experience engagement) because they just allow us to do our job.

Think of these needs in terms of Maslow's famous hierarchy. On the bottom are our most basic needs; if they are not fulfilled, we are generally not very concerned with the needs that are higher on the hierarchy. For example, if we don't have food and shelter, that's likely to create stress and decrease the likelihood of concerns about achieving great things at work. In fact, more recent variations of the hierarchy of needs actually distinguish between the lower-level needs, calling them "deficiency" needs, and the higher-level needs, calling them "growth" needs. Those lower-level needs are generally more clearly understood and common across people. As we move up the hierarchy, the needs start to become more nebulous with more variety of meanings among people. As a result, probably the bigger challenge with engagement, in comparison to the challenges that burnout presents, is that engagement requires a greater acknowledgment of the individualized relationship with resources.

Digging into research on what causes burnout can lead down one heck of a rabbit hole. To keep things manageable, I'll focus on two ways of thinking about resources that lead to engagement: (1) resources may be connected in ways that make them more or less effective (resource caravans) and (2) you as a leader can create the conditions that can bring the most effective resources together (resource passageways). These two ways of thinking about resources will be particularly helpful as we start to explore strategies for intervention.

Resource Caravans

If you were to study your most engaged employees, you likely would find some common resources that occur together among those employees. When those resources are not found together and possibly even conflict, engagement is far less likely. For example, Trougakos and colleagues (2014) studied lunch and social breaks at work. They found that those breaks are a resource but are only effective if employees can choose what they do during their breaks. Some of my work with colleagues at the University of Alabama found a similar effect with family-friendly workplace policies such as on-site childcare (Mandeville, Halbesleben, and Whitman 2016). In a study of first responders and nurses, we found that merely offering such policies doesn't necessarily lead to employees using their benefits and thus, they aren't really resources.

Perhaps the most intuitive example of resource caravans is the combination of ability, incentives, and time. If you think about times when you have been most engaged in a task, almost certainly you knew what you were doing (ability), were motivated to engage in it and attain a valued outcome (incentives), and could get to it (time). Could you complete a task, and maybe even be immersed in it, with only one or two of those resources in place? I suppose so. But a high degree of engagement in your work is most likely to be realized when all three are in place. If even one is missing or barely there, you may still give some effort, but I doubt you would label that effort as "engaged."

With that in mind, the key to engaging employees is finding that combination of resources that leads to optimal engagement and then setting up the conditions for those resources to occur together. While the resources may take different forms depending on the needs of the individual, it's helpful to start with a combination of ability, incentives, and time with the goal of understanding what each of those resources means for each situation. For example, when we talk about an employee's ability to do something, we often speak in terms of whether they know what to do and how to do it. For some employees, a lack of knowledge about what and how is the key limitation to their ability. In healthcare, however, the absence of that form of ability probably is not limiting an employee's engagement. Instead, they may be facing another barrier to getting the job done in the way they know it should be done.

This idea leads us back to the concept of work-arounds covered in chapter 1. Recall that a work-around is an alternative procedure undertaken to circumvent a block in workflow. It limits an employee's ability to do their job and is tied to the way the work is designed. One could argue that work-arounds are actually creative solutions to problems, but employees would prefer not to have to engage in work-arounds.

Calling work-arounds a manifestation of engagement is a stretch. In fact, healthcare providers blame barriers that require work-arounds for keeping them from being engaged in their work (Barrett 2020). Even if healthcare providers have the incentive and time to provide high-quality care, poorly designed systems will limit their ability to deliver it. However, if ability, incentive, and time are all in alignment, work-arounds typically are not necessary. Employees can instead be free to engage in work that adds value to their patients and their organization.

Resource Passageways

To identify and implement resource caravans, organizations must create the conditions that create and support what Hobfoll (2011) called *resource passageways*. It is up to leaders to set up the conditions for those resources to emerge, an effort that requires a number of specific leadership behaviors.

Research on leadership's impact on employee engagement is quite extensive. It will come as little surprise that more positive leadership behaviors (e.g., providing encouragement and social support) are more likely to lead to engagement than negative behaviors (e.g., abusive supervision). But even focusing on positive leadership can overwhelm when encountering broad approaches such as transformational, ethical, authentic, and servant leadership, plus specific behaviors such as trust building, coaching, and empowerment. They all seem like good things, but they are a lot to manage at once.

It might be helpful to narrow the findings down to a few common themes that can be translated into action. Two threads run through nearly all of the positive leadership approaches and behaviors:

- **Help employees see where they fit in with the bigger picture.** This can come in the form of presenting a vision, explaining how their work contributes to achieving overall organizational goals, setting expectations, and providing feedback. Employees who are engaged are proud of their work, feel that it is meaningful, and want to contribute to something bigger than themselves. If they don't understand the bigger picture and how they fit in, what are they actually engaged with?

- **Take an authentic interest in the success of employees.** This may be involve providing them with the tools and resources to do their job. But once those are in place, it likely involves understanding what success means to them, involving them in decisions that drive their success, and celebrating when they are successful.

Chapter 5 will get into more details about how to implement these two ideas in your workplace. For now, it's important to understand the role you can play in providing the resources employees need to be engaged.

TAKEAWAY POINTS: ENGAGEMENT IS OUR GOAL

As we seek to reduce burnout and improve our healthcare organizations, our end goal is to enhance engagement among our employees. The following points summarize the ground covered in this chapter:

- There are various perspectives on engagement. Some emphasize the psychological state of engagement, while others consider the behaviors or conditions that lead to engagement. Both perspectives have value; they just focus on different aspects of engagement.
- Engagement is a positive outcome for both employees and organizations, leading to valuable outcomes such as improved performance, better quality of care, a safer work environment, and creativity.
- The processes that underly the experience of burnout also help to explain the experience of engagement. In

particular, engagement is the result of having adequate resources to navigate one's job, such as ability, incentives, and time.

We are getting closer to the point where we can address stress and burnout among healthcare professionals. However, as with any intervention, such efforts must be supported with data. Otherwise, the work will be misguided. The next chapter discusses the myriad ways to assess stress and burnout in healthcare and provides the tools you will need to get a handle on the extent of the problem in your organization.

FURTHER READING

Truss, C., R. Delbridge, K. Alfes, A. Shantz, and E. Soane (eds.). 2013. *Employee Engagement in Theory and Practice*. London: Routledge.

West, M., and J. Dawson. 2012. *Employee Engagement and NHS Performance*. London: King's Fund.

CHAPTER 4

Measuring Stress, Burnout, and Engagement

There are days that I feel already tired before I go to work.
—Item from the Oldenburg Burnout Inventory,
intended to measure exhaustion

ASSESSING STRESS, BURNOUT, and engagement is not as easy as it may seem at first. Think about what you have read in this book so far. How would *you* assess stress? Simple mechanisms for measuring these concepts are not obvious. The question, "Are you stressed?" is an ineffective gauge. People may not know what it means to be stressed, or they may have their own idiosyncratic definition. As you learned in previous chapters, everybody experiences stress differently.

Good data are needed to move forward with intervention efforts. If we don't know how much stress people are experiencing or, more important, their sources of stress, we will have a difficult time reducing it. Moreover, if we want to evaluate our intervention later, we will need a consistent way to assess stress over time. This chapter introduces a variety of options for assessing stress and burnout, focusing on some of the more popular, feasible techniques for healthcare professionals.

ASSESSING STRESS

Historically, a checklist of common dramatic life events (e.g., marriage, divorce, new job, death in the family), called the Social Readjustment Scale, was most commonly used to assess stress (Holmes and Rahe 1967). Each event was given a numeric score (e.g., death of a spouse is 100; divorce is 73; vacation is 13). The higher a person's score, the more stress they were experiencing. While this approach is intuitive, its problem is twofold. First, stress theories argue that stress is experienced within a context. For example, a death in the family could be a welcome end to a long, difficult struggle with cancer and relieve someone from significant caretaking responsibilities. Likewise, in some cases, the scale didn't differentiate between voluntary and involuntary stressors (e.g., initiating a divorce vs. receiving notice that one's spouse filed for divorce). For these reasons, someone can take on a new job, get married, or experience any number of other things and not seem as stressed as someone else because those events may have brought about welcome improvements to that person's previous plight.

Second, the scale was based on major life events. In most cases, pervasive, everyday hassles—as opposed to momentous occurrences—are more commonly the types of stressors that lead to burnout. Perhaps the infusion pump isn't working correctly, or overtime has been made involuntary for the week because of a staff shortage. These types of issues were not reflected in the life events scale, yet they have a profound impact on employees' experiences of stress and strain. In short, the scale lacked sensitivity; someone could have been experiencing high levels of stress at work, but because they did not check off any of the major events listed, they registered low on the stress scale.

In seeking more "objective" approaches to assessing stress, some have advocated for the use of tests that take physiological measures ranging from heart rate to blood cortisol levels. These approaches are somewhat valuable, and there is a host of evidence to support their role in the stress process, but they also have drawbacks. Until recently, physiological measures of stress were difficult to collect, often requiring blood draws that would not be feasible for use within organizations. That may change as research continues to grow rapidly, validating the use of "wearables" to detect stress primarily through measurement of heart rate variability. However, a recent systematic study from a team of Australian researchers suggests we are still years away from being confident in the reliability of off-the-shelf smart devices for this purpose (Hickey et al. 2021).

Once we get to that point, it is still unclear how helpful those sensors will be. In most cases, the goal is to understand and address *why* employees have these physiological responses, not the responses themselves. Knowing that an employee has high cortisol levels, or a specific heart rate variability pattern, may be a marker that they are stressed, but it does not tell us much about what caused those markers. As a result, we are largely right back at the start in terms of designing any kind of intervention.

Various measures have been created to assess the stressors relevant to healthcare professionals. The Nursing Stress Scale (NSS) has been predominant in the nursing literature (Gray-Toft and Anderson 1981). Widely used in research, this scale has been translated from English into a number of languages, including Spanish and Chinese. In essence, the NSS is a nursing-specific variant of the life event scale that measures stress according to the frequency of stressful events. Since its inception, it has been expanded to capture nine sources of stress in the nursing profession, along with the frequency of each source (see French et al. 2000). This scale has been commonly criticized for neglecting to take into account the resources available to the respondent to address the stressors, similar to the concerns with life events checklists. The applicability of the NSS to healthcare occupations beyond nursing is also questionable.

An alternative approach is to capture the respondent's overall feeling of stress. Instead of focusing on resources, this approach builds the appraisal of demands into the assessment questions. Cohen and colleagues' (1983) Perceived Stress Scale (PSS) is one example of a tool that takes this approach. The PSS and other similar scales are more useful in that they are general enough to apply to most occupations and tend to return highly valid results. The general nature of these scales' assessment questions, however, makes diagnosis of specific stressors difficult. For example, consider this question: "In the last month, how often have you felt that you were effectively coping with important changes occurring in your life?" Would responses to such a question help pinpoint what needs to be "fixed" to reduce stress in the workplace? Not likely.

The bottom line is that an ideal measure of stress has yet to be designed. The key is to understand whom you are assessing and what you are seeking to measure. If you are trying to get an overall feel for the level of stress in your facility, the PSS may help you gather the information you need to do so. If you want to diagnose specific stressors among professionals of a specific occupation, then a scale similar to the NSS would work better. No matter what you choose, keep in mind that there is no perfect tool for measuring stress among healthcare professionals.

ASSESSING BURNOUT

Although somewhat easier to measure than stress, burnout is similarly difficult to assess. Historically, it has been measured using pencil-and-paper surveys. Following are descriptions of some of the options available including how they approach burnout and their advantages and disadvantages. Many measures have been developed, but their use may be questionable if there is no evidence supporting their effectiveness. For brevity, the discussion covers methods that have produced reliable and valid results. Their outcomes are consistent over time and across items, and they measure what they say they measure.

The Maslach Burnout Inventory

The Maslach Burnout Inventory (MBI), created by Maslach and Jackson (1981), is by far the most-used measure. It is based on

Maslach's three-dimensional conceptualization of burnout, which includes subscales for emotional exhaustion, depersonalization (called *cynicism* in the most recent iteration), and reduced personal efficacy. This measure has been translated into dozens of languages. It is available in several versions including a traditional version for service providers, a general version that does not refer to specific clients and can be applied to nearly any profession, and a version for educators. In recent years, more specific variations of the original measures have been introduced that are better suited for healthcare professionals and students.

The MBI asks the respondent to indicate the frequency with which a series of statements apply to them. Because of its popularity, a great deal of attention has been paid to testing the MBI's reliability and validity. It withstands these tests well; the three subscales emerge as distinct factors. Moreover, it adequately discriminates between burnout and other related measures such as depression.

Despite its common use, the MBI has drawn criticism. The usefulness of its personal efficacy scale is questionable, as it tends not to work as consistently as the other two dimensions. Because it is a commercial test, the MBI involves a cost to administer; organizations have to purchase a license to from Mind Garden, the test's publisher (see www.mindgarden.com). In a large health system, this expense could add up quickly, though there are volume discounts, and the cost is lower if one is using the MBI for research purposes.

The measure's construction poses another problem. All of the items are phrased in the same direction (the respondent's burnout score increases each time they answer a statement affirmatively). People may figure out this pattern and respond without really thinking about the statements. For example, when faced with long surveys, people may repeatedly select the same response (e.g., always select "1"), regardless of how they really feel. Or they may read the first few questions, realize they are all about the same topic, and respond similarly to all questions on the inventory without really thinking about them.

The Oldenburg Burnout Inventory

To address the concerns about cost and structure, and recognizing the limitations of the personal efficacy scale, Demerouti and colleagues (2002) developed the Oldenburg Burnout Inventory (OLBI), which assesses burnout on the basis of two dimensions: emotional exhaustion and disengagement. (The quote at the start of the chapter is a sample item from the exhaustion subscale of the OLBI.) It is free to use for noncommercial purposes. It also addresses the MBI's structure issue by balancing positively and negatively worded items so respondents cannot lapse into an answer pattern but must carefully consider each statement. Originally developed in German, the OLBI has been translated into many languages, validated in peer-reviewed journals, and applies to any occupation; it does not specifically refer to working with customers or patients.

Structured similarly to the MBI, the OLBI includes 16 statements that require responses. Rather than emphasizing the frequency with which the respondent experiences each item, the OLBI asks respondents to indicate the extent to which they agree with the statement. This type of scaling (*strongly agree* to *strongly disagree*) corresponds with many other measures, so it can be consistent when embedded with other measures in a larger survey.

The reliability and validity of the OLBI have also been studied, and it has held up well. A number of studies have compared the OLBI directly to the MBI, finding sufficient conceptual overlap between the emotional exhaustion and depersonalization/disengagement/cynicism dimensions of the OLBI and MBI.

Other Measures of Burnout

The MBI and OBI are by far the most common measures used to assess burnout in the research literature and in the field. However, I'll briefly note two others.

The Copenhagen Burnout Inventory, developed by Kristensen and colleagues (2005), expands the domain of burnout beyond work to include personal burnout, work-related burnout, and client-related burnout. The idea is to customize the measure to fit the situation of the respondents who are completing the items. For example, if they don't work with clients, there is no need to measure that subsection.

The Staff Burnout Scale for Health Professionals (SBS-HP), as its name suggests, is intended specifically for the healthcare sector (Jones 1980). The SBS-HP measures burnout on the basis of adverse cognitive, affective, behavioral, and psychophysical reactions. Although it has the potential advantage of being tailored to health-care settings, the SBS-HP does not have the same track record as the measures discussed earlier and its conceptualization of burnout centered on four adverse reactions is inconsistent with much of the literature on the topic.

ASSESSING ENGAGEMENT

The measurement of engagement shares several characteristics with the common measures of stress and burnout. While some options employ formats like checklists to assess conditions underlying engagement, others attempt to measure the psychological processes of engagement. The approach you take with the assessment of engagement depends somewhat on what you are trying to accomplish. As noted in chapter 3, there are two main perspectives on engagement (psychologically focused and management focused); the two most common measures of engagement reflect each of those perspectives.

Gallup Q12

Among the first measures of employee engagement was the Gallup Workplace Audit (Gallup Organization 1992), now called the

Gallup Q^{12}. As its name implies, it purports to cover 12 needs of employees that, when met, will lead to engagement. This measure is similar to the checklist approach to stress; however, rather than focus on whether something has occurred, the Q^{12} emphasizes conditions that would potentially lead to engagement.

One could argue that this measure fits conservation of resources theory very well, as the conditions measured by the Q^{12} are indicators that employees have resources to draw upon to engage with their work. With that in mind, the Q^{12} can be useful if you focus a little less on the extent to which people are engaged in your organization and more on whether the work environment supports engagement.

A drawback of the Q^{12} is that it is a commercial product of the Gallup Organization. The costs can be rather high, especially for a small group. In 2022, the cost of the Q^{12} was $15 per participant, with volume discounts for more than 100 participants. The cost does include additional resources that may be of value, such as benchmarking with other organizations. Like other commercial measures, Gallup claims its measure is reliable and valid. Peer reviews to support those claims are a bit harder to come by, though some data are available (e.g., Harter et al. 2010).

Utrecht Work Engagement Scale

By far, the most common measure of engagement in the academic literature is the Utrecht Work Engagement Scale (UWES) created by Wilmar Schaufeli and colleagues (2002). The UWES measures the psychological experience of engagement, including subscales for vigor, dedication, and absorption facets (discussed in chapter 3). This 17-item scale has been translated into many languages and validated in a large number of peer-reviewed publications. Researchers have adapted the scale for special populations such as students (e.g., Carmona-Halty, Schaufeli, and Salanova 2019).

The UWES is probably a fine option if money is an issue, as it is available without cost. Also, the UWES is useful if you are more interested in measuring the degree of engagement of your employees than in measuring the conditions that can lead to engagement. However, the UWES may be less useful when it comes time to translate your data into interventions. The items refer more to states of being. For example, if a work unit scored an average of 2 out of 5 on the item "At my work, I feel that I am bursting with energy," what would you do next?

Other Measures of Engagement

Many consulting firms have created their own proprietary engagement measures. Further, other measures have been described in peer-reviewed articles that purport to assess engagement. The differences in these scales reflect differing perspectives on the concept of engagement. For example, the 12-item Shirom-Melamed Vigor Measure (Shirom 2008) concentrates on the vigor facet of engagement, though it divides vigor into physical, emotional, and cognitive components. Bruce Rich and colleagues (2010) came up with a measure for the physical, emotional, and cognitive components of engagement. A measure developed by Thomas Britt and colleagues (2005) includes four items that emphasize performance and commitment elements of the job.

My fellow academics generally justify their creation of new measures of engagement with the assertion that others do not fully measure engagement, even while using the same foundational views of what engagement is. I have gone into less detail on these alternative measures largely because they are used much less frequently in the academic literature and, from what I can tell, in the field.

RECOMMENDATIONS ON THE LENGTH OF ASSESSMENTS

One concern that frequently comes up when I'm working with an organization to collect data concerns the length of the survey.

Many burnout and engagement measures require respondents to complete 15 to 30 items for each component of burnout or engagement (e.g., emotional exhaustion). When considering length of surveys, researchers frequently follow a rule of thumb of 4 items per minute. Typically, people don't use that much time, but that rule captures the vast majority of people completing your survey. If all you are measuring is burnout, or maybe burnout and engagement, you might be fine with the scales as they were designed. However, in many cases we want to capture other information, which will require a longer survey. Particularly if we are concerned that burnout may be a problem in our organization, using a long survey may not be optimal.

Fortunately, you have options. In some cases, researchers have created and tested the validity and reliability of shortened versions of the scale. For example, while the full version of the UWES is 17 items, a 9-item version is available with adequate validity and reliability data to support its use (see Schaufeli, Bakker, and Salanova 2006). More recently, researchers at the University of Alabama tested and found support for the use of a three-item version of the UWES (Matthews, Mills, and Wise 2020) that may be especially attractive if you want to capture frequent, short check-ins with employees to identify changes in engagement over time.

Another approach is to measure more specific facets of burnout and engagement. Because, for example, many believe that exhaustion is the first facet of burnout to manifest, leading to disengagement and reduced personal efficacy, researchers typically suggest measuring only exhaustion. This is the approach I have frequently used in my own work, using either the five-item exhaustion subscale of the MBI or the eight-item exhaustion subscale of the OLBI. As the authors of the MBI note, however, if you are more interested in assessing the point where you might truly consider someone "burned out," it might make more sense to only capture the depersonalization/disengagement/cynicism subscales. Taking this approach is a little less clear for engagement because the three facets of engagement are not temporally structured in quite the same way as burnout.

However, I have seen people concentrate on one or two facets, particularly if there is interest in specific facets.

TAKEAWAY POINTS: GATHERING THE DATA YOU NEED

Although we have some good options for assessing stress and burnout, we don't have one easy, perfect solution. Here are important points to take away from this chapter:

- Stress is exceedingly difficult to measure. There are various imperfect ways to measure stress, and the best tool for the job will depend on the context in which the stress is experienced.
- Measures of burnout are somewhat more consistent than measures of stress. There are important advantages and disadvantages to each.
- Measures of engagement largely take on two forms that are similar to measures of stress and burnout, respectively. They are (1) measures of conditions that should lead to engagement and (2) measures that assess the psychological state of engagement.
- To select an appropriate measure for your situation, you may need to consider shortened versions of the scales or determine which dimensions of construct you wish to assess (e.g., only measuring emotional exhaustion for burnout).

Well, you now have all the background information on stress, burnout, and engagement. Chapter 5 explores solutions to the stress epidemic in healthcare by addressing existing burnout and discussing prevention of additional burnout.

CHAPTER 5

The BRIDGES Program: Reducing Stress and Burnout in Healthcare Professionals

If management knew how to do our jobs so well, why would they need to make changes to them all the time to make them "easier"? I know how to do my job, and if they bothered to ask, I'd tell them how I could do it better.

—Maintenance worker at a long-term care facility

I know that [administration] may not be able to implement all the changes we are recommending. We all understand that. Honestly, they've already taken a huge step by listening and involving us in the process.

—Psychiatrist in a university-based student health clinic

AT THIS POINT, let's take a moment to see where we are in our journey. I started by making the case for why you should address stress and burnout in your healthcare organization. I have defined stress, burnout, and engagement and explained the dynamics underlying them. This discussion provided a basis from which to structure interventions. Chapter 4 discussed tools for measuring stress and burnout that can help evaluate the extent of the problem and the success of an intervention.

This chapter introduces techniques for reducing stress and burnout. It will present the acute phase of addressing issues in your organization. Next, chapter 6 will describe the longer-term maintenance so you can avoid having to come back to this chapter again. Consider this analogy: Imagine you just had a heart attack. You will require intensive treatment, perhaps an angioplasty, to address the blockage. But does that procedure solve the problem? Upon discharge, will the physician say, "Come on back when you need to be fixed again"? Hopefully not. Instead, you will be given advice on dietary and lifestyle changes to sustain a healthy body. In terms of the metaphor, this chapter is the angioplasty—its purpose is to clear out the problem. Chapter 6 will delve into more detail on the "lifestyle changes" that will help maintain a less stressful environment.

TARGETING THE INDIVIDUAL VERSUS TARGETING THE ENVIRONMENT

One of two main approaches can be taken when developing intervention programs to address burnout: We can try to treat the individual, or we can try to change the environment in which that individual works. The former is tempting. Everyone experiences stress differently, so why not focus on the individual to address it?

The aim of many individual-focused programs is to help the employee build coping abilities that will enable them to address the underlying stressors that are leading to burnout. These programs may involve training to improve skills such as time management, interpersonal relations, stress inoculation, and assertiveness. Or they may help employees step away from the stress of work temporarily via vacationing, deep breathing, meditation, and even squeezing stress balls. They are attractive because they seem to fit any situation. No matter what the stressor is, wouldn't time management address it at some level?

The Limitations of "Treating" an Individual

The evaluation of individual-focused programs has been mixed. They may reduce burnout temporarily or reduce specific symptoms of burnout, especially for employees whose problem truly was a lack of skills to handle difficulties with work and for those experiencing the worst stress at the time of intervention. For example, Brazier and colleagues (2022) found that a simple text messaging intervention did not reduce burnout or improve well-being in their overall sample of anesthesiology trainees, but it did reduce burnout among those who had indicated a particularly high negative impact from the COVID-19 pandemic.

There is also evidence that meditation or mindfulness training can put bodies in a better position to deal with stress. However, this training does not address the underlying cause of the burnout—stressors at work—and therefore is unlikely to reduce burnout over the long term. Teaching people to cope may work for a while, but eventually they will face stressors they aren't equipped to handle. Such training also can be very time-intensive for healthcare professionals and require very specific trainers to implement. It may come as little surprise that "burnout or stress management seminars" were the least likely of several interventions to be considered "very effective" in a study of urologists conducted by a team led by Poone Shoureshi (2022).

These individual-focused programs also assume that employees have never thought to manage their time better or improve their assertiveness. In many cases, they may have wanted to try these techniques, but they simply didn't work in their situation. Time management doesn't make tasks disappear.

Perhaps the most compelling reason these programs don't work is the high turnover in healthcare organizations. Think about it: You could spend a lot of effort and money training your nursing staff using one of the approaches described here. Then, in the next year, 20 percent of them leave the organization. The year after, another

20 percent leave. After a few years, you have to start over, and the stressors are all still there.

The Effectiveness of an Environmental Approach

Programs that target changes to the stressful environment are generally more successful in reducing stress than programs that focus on the individual. For example, studies of alternative work schedules (e.g., Ali et al. 2011), restructuring of roles and care models (Reid et al. 2010), and work process improvements coupled with accountability for senior leadership (Dunn et al. 2007) have shown a positive impact on burnout. At least two meta-analyses have examined the impact of organization-based interventions compared to individual-based interventions on reducing physician burnout, and they have found that organization-based interventions are more effective (Panagioti et al. 2017; West et al. 2016). A report from the National Academy of Medicine Action Collaborative on Clinician Well-Being and Resilience (Sinsky et al. 2020) provides a useful table summarizing some of the approaches that have been taken.

That said, interventions still must be carefully designed to ensure they meet the needs of the group they are intended to support. As Wiederhold and colleagues (2018) concluded in their systematic review of interventions to reduce physician burnout, characteristics of the group play a key role in successful interventions.

As this discussion has shown, there is no catch-all solution to the burnout problem. However, there is a general *framework* for addressing stress and burnout. It is based on a critically important point I presented in the introduction to this book: People want to be involved in the changes that happen in their jobs. Since writing the first edition of this book, there has been increasing advocacy for involvement of healthcare professionals in the design of healthcare interventions (see Ward et al. 2018; West et al. 2016) based on evidence that doing so reduces burnout and increases engagement. One compelling example from the Mayo Clinic used a process similar to what I'll describe in this chapter to involve physicians and allied health staff, with significant reductions in burnout and increases in engagement (Swensen, Kabcenell, and Shanafelt 2016).

Employees are an amazing source of ideas. If they are given an opportunity to share those ideas, they will be even more engaged with their work and committed to seeing their ideas through. All these factors figure into a technique called *action research*.

ACTION RESEARCH AS A BURNOUT-REDUCING MECHANISM

Action research (sometimes called *participatory action research* or *action learning*) is an empirical and reflective process by which employees (in our case, healthcare professionals) work toward solutions to an organization's problems by focusing on the positive aspects of their experiences. This process is widely accepted in organization development and management consulting and has experienced a significant resurgence in organizational theory and research. Rather than treating employees as a problem that needs to be solved, employees become the generator of solutions to the challenges at work.

I was introduced to action research early in my career while working on a consulting project with a federal fire department (see Halbesleben, Osburn, and Mumford 2006). The employees of the department were experiencing high degrees of stress following the events of September 11, 2001. At the time, I had never used action research, but given my limited experience with the fire service, I was not in the best position to provide "expert recommendations." As I read more about action research, I became more convinced that it was the most appropriate strategy for the situation. Over time, I've come to realize it has tremendous power to address stress and burnout in a lot of situations.

There are various action research techniques. All are based on similar principles. First, the subjects of the research (employees) need to be deeply embedded in the process, not just "involved."

Managers commonly pass out surveys or conduct formal or informal focus groups to gauge their employees' sentiments before designing interventions. For example, a manager might pass out a staff satisfaction survey, discover that the department's physicians are unhappy with policies regarding operating room scheduling, and make some changes to the operating room schedule. The subjects of the research are certainly involved in the process, but they are not deeply embedded in it. *Deeply embedded* means they helped design the survey and collect the data. It means they came up with the concerns *and* the solutions. It means they carried out the solutions (with their manager's support and resources). It means they were involved in evaluating the process downstream. Overall, it means the managers are giving up a lot of power for the good of all involved.

> In action research, subjects (or employees or stakeholders) are not just involved in the process; they are deeply embedded in it.

A second hallmark of action research programs is an action/reflection cycle, similar to Deming's Plan-Do-Study-Act (or Shewhart's Plan-Do-Check-Act) quality improvement cycle. This cycle elaborates on the action/reflection concept, which involves trying different solutions to problems, reflecting on them, and then trying something different.

There are several different ways to engage in an action/reflection cycle. Exhibit 5.1 illustrates how the cycle might play out early in the process (before implementation of solutions). The idea is to hold initial meetings with stakeholders to elicit ideas about what is happening. These meetings are followed by reflection about the elicited ideas and integration with the evidence. For example, if social support seems to be a concern among your employees, you could look at the evidence regarding the best sources of social support and the best forms of support. Then, you could observe the work environment and engage employees in informal discussion. On the basis of these observations and discussions, you could elaborate on how support might play a role in the environment. After further reflection, you could conduct interviews with employees. After yet more reflection, you could conduct a survey and use quantitative data to elaborate further.

These sources of information or action are not set in stone; you can substitute whatever you feel is appropriate for the situation. Perhaps you can gather better information through focus groups. The point is that you are taking some action—in this case, collecting information—and then reflecting on how you might use that information.

Beyond the deep embedding of stakeholders and the action/reflection cycles, different action research programs part ways on the details of implementation. In this chapter, I will propose a

Exhibit 5.1 Example of the Action/Reflection Process in Action Research

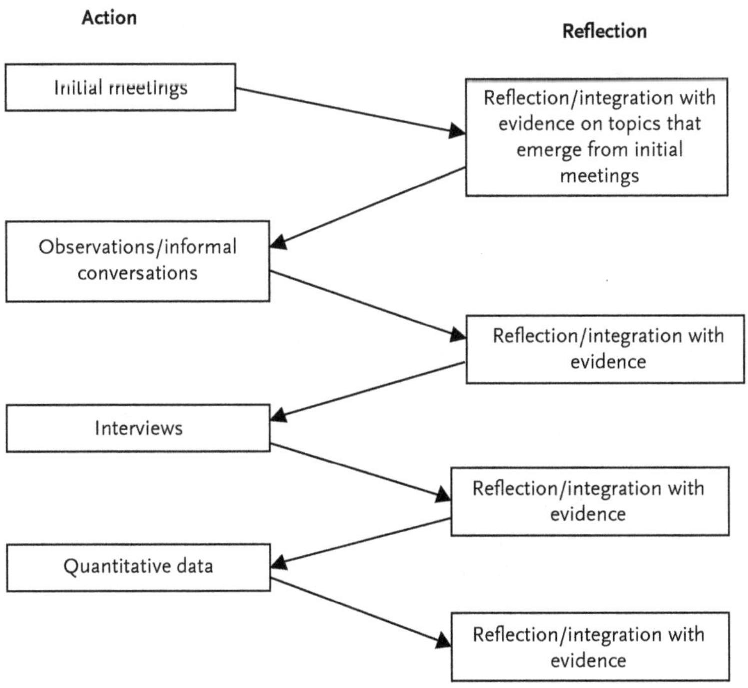

customizable framework that merges many of the ideas proposed in the action research literature. I have distilled these ideas into a model program that seems to work best for addressing issues of stress and burnout in the workplace.

INTRODUCING BRIDGES

The BRIDGES program stands for **B**uild **R**elationships, **I**dentify, **D**esign, **G**ive it a try, **E**valuate, and **S**ustain. The acronym makes the program easier to remember. It is also symbolic. In 2001, the Institute of Medicine released *Crossing the Quality Chasm: A New Health System for the 21st Century*. Arguably, one of the ways to bridge this chasm is to develop a workforce that is not burned out but instead engaged in providing safe, high-quality care. This program attempts to build that bridge.

More generally, it is central to the stress-strain metaphor. In chapter 2, you learned that in engineering terms, stress is the momentary pressure placed on a structure (such as a bridge). When that structure starts to deteriorate, it is strained. Further, the acronym refers to the bridges you are going to build between your employees. A goal of this program is to help you develop a support network that will reduce the negative impact of stress. These "bridges" might be the most important structures you develop in your work.

BRIDGES follows a cycle of four steps (see exhibit 5.2). The next few sections describe each step and how it can be implemented to reduce burnout in your organization.

Step 1: Build Relationships

Extensive efforts to build relationships must be made in action research programs. While better relationships are an *outcome* of action research, their development is an important first step in the process. If you don't build strong relationships, your employees

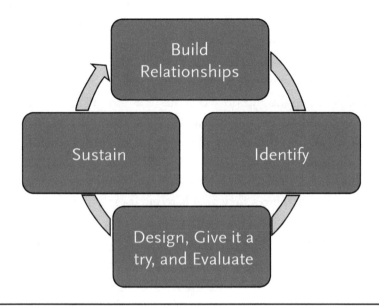

won't trust you enough to share their ideas. They won't feel as though you are willing to support their ideas. They will hesitate to take responsibility for implementing ideas because they will worry that they are being set up for failure.

Keep in mind how consulting projects usually work. Management brings in an outsider and tells everyone, "Here's the consultant. They are going to address our problems." As we saw in the classic 1999 film *Office Space,* employees do not react favorably to consultants. They see them as people brought in to fire staff or tell them how they are underperforming in their jobs.

I've overcome this stigma in a variety of ways. While the fire-fighting project mentioned earlier is not a healthcare example, it illustrates an interesting approach to changing this perception. I did the obvious things, such as going out on calls with firefighters, but what really made the difference was my effort to learn as much about the job as I could. I cooked. I watched football with them.

I helped wash fire trucks. I even slept in the fire station for a few nights. I wore a uniform (just around the station, of course). These gestures broke down the barriers between us. They came to see me as a guy who was trying to learn as much about the job as he could so he could help them.

In healthcare, I make similar efforts. I don't just show up during the day shift when it's convenient for me. I stop by units in the middle of the night and on weekends. I engage in small talk and ask to see pictures of staff members' kids. I always explain why I am there and that I'm not trying to pester them. In general, I try to build a connection so they feel comfortable, and then find out what stresses them on the job by asking them to share some of their worst work experiences. My goal is to elicit great ideas about how their work experience could be better. The only way I'm going to achieve that goal is by showing them that they can safely share their thoughts with me.

My job is easier than a manager's job in this regard, because while I may be a stranger to these people, I don't have the baggage that comes with being part of management. For example, in some of the situations I encounter, there is little trust in management because employees perceive that management is unwilling to make real changes. This mindset can be a significant obstacle. So, let's look at some ways to address that problem.

First, managers need to be more visible. With all that managers have going on in their jobs, finding the time to chat with people can be difficult. Despite the difficulty in finding the time, it really is important in order to successfully implement changes. Second, managers need to take an authentic interest in people's ideas. People have to feel comfortable confiding in their manager and should want to work with them. Small wins play a big role here.

Being more visible and sincere and taking people's ideas seriously are not new ideas. Packaged as a concept called *individualized consideration,* the ideas have been at the forefront of the leadership literature for years. Telling people to do these things is like telling people to lose weight. They want to lose weight and know what they need to do (exercise and consume fewer calories), yet they can't manage to implement a plan of action. They simply don't make weight loss a priority. Similarly, to effectively reduce stress you need to take this step seriously. The rest of this book is irrelevant if you don't build relationships. Let's explore relationship building in more detail.

Be Visible

Start by carving out time *each day* to walk around your facility. Visit two units per day. Vary the times so you can hit multiple shifts (including the night shift—many interventions have derailed because the manager did not fully consider the implications for *all* staff, just those working during the day). On each unit, select at least one person and connect. Ask that person how their day is going, and ask a personal question (not too personal, of course) to find common ground. Then ask that person about what stresses them at work and what would make their job easier.

When chatting with staff members, be sensitive to what they are doing at the time. Remember: The goal is to reduce their stress, not make it worse. When I interviewed intensive care unit nurses, for example, I tried not to catch them as they were walking quickly out of a patient room and to a computer. They were likely going to place an order or enter other information that they might forget. A more appropriate time would be when they are charting, but first ask whether they can chat for a moment when they are done with the chart.

Visits must become a habit—something done with regular intervals, at least monthly. If you can visit units more often or visit more than two units, all the better. Eventually, people will recognize that you are with them in the trenches. You'll become aware of the stressors they experience daily. If you don't proactively visit and chat with staff, you'll hear about only larger issues that have escalated to your suite, and by that point, the situation may be too difficult to turn around.

If this approach sounds familiar, it is sometimes called "walk-rounds." Initially centered on patient safety, an emerging body of research from Duke University is finding that walkrounds are also effective in reducing burnout and increasing engagement (see Sexton et al. 2018, 2021).

Clearly, the notion of freely walking around units in most clinical settings is made a bit more challenging by a highly contagious virus. However, organizations have adapted their walkround to account for COVID-19 and have even used walkrounds to directly address well-being of healthcare workers and generate ideas for controlling infection spread within their organizations (Gintoli et al. 2021; Wu et al., 2020). The Dell Medical School at the University of Texas continued its walkrounds to identify solutions to challenges like obtaining oxygen and pulse oximeters when discharging COVID-19 patients (Moriates et al. 2022).

Take an Authentic Interest in People's Ideas

Healthcare leaders must take an authentic interest in their staff's ideas by truly listening to those ideas and posing meaningful questions to learn more. Ask people for their ideas. Tell the interviewees about some of the great ideas you have heard; ask what they think of them. Share your own ideas, and then see whether they are still valid after the interviewees provide their feedback. You demonstrate genuine interest when you flesh out ideas this way. Ask for clarification on details. How might the idea work? Who might be affected?

Be careful not to play devil's advocate at this stage. Don't point out all of the idea's flaws and the ways it might not work. Ideas should be vetted, tested, and evaluated later in the process. No matter how unrealistic or poor their ideas are, the goal at this point is to get staff to feel comfortable sharing them with you. When you react positively to abstract notions, you encourage people to share ideas that are less obvious and less "safe"—precursors to the development of innovative approaches.

Shoot for small wins. Try a few of the easier and less controversial ideas. Implement them quickly to build momentum. Momentum is of utmost importance in these types of situations. While you certainly need to be thoughtful as you move forward, too much thinking can kill the momentum of interventions. Solutions can be refined throughout the process, so moving forward with some simple ideas is not overly risky.

As with walkrounds, a stream of research led by Canadian researcher Heather Laschinger supports the idea that being authentic as a leader reduces burnout and increases engagement (see Laschinger et al. 2015, 2016). In fact, the American Association of Critical-Care Nurses (2005) identified authentic leadership as vital to healthy work environments. These findings are consistent with suggestions that engaging physicians in problem-solving can be an important way to reduce their burnout (Shanafelt et al. 2015).

Keys to Building Relationships in Action Research

Visibility
Authentic interest in people's ideas

Over time, these steps will go a long way on the road to establishing trust. People will start to recognize that something is up. Someone cares about them as professionals. Someone is listening to their ideas and hoping they will share more ideas. Frankly, these are good things regardless of what you are trying to address. Nonetheless, let's continue in the BRIDGES model with the next step.

Step 2: Identify

In this step, the relationships built in step 1 are leveraged to generate the ideas you need to solve the stress problem in your facility. Identification occurs in three phases: team identification, identification of challenges (in this case, stressors), and identification of opportunities to reduce burnout. Before changes can be made, you need to determine what the organization's problems are and the opportunities for change that are open to you.

Identify Your Team

Building on the basis of your visits and chats, identify employees who show particular interest in the initiative to address stress and burnout. They may be important resources as you move forward. Any cause needs champions. As you identify your team, keep the following points in mind:

- Don't default to other people in management or others with formal titles. Remember that there is a difference between leadership and management; you need leaders, not managers. You want the people whom employees go to when they have questions and concerns, who naturally engage others, and whom others listen to when things get hairy. You'll find that, in many cases, these people are not in management positions. Downey, Parslow, and Smart (2011) suggest informal nurse leaders are an underused "hidden treasure."

- Don't include those too high in the ranks, either. I've learned this firsthand since I became dean of a college. It turns out my ideas became the best possible direction for the college the moment I became dean (kidding, of course). I have had to be increasingly thoughtful about which meetings to attend and now avoid meetings where the initial ideas are going to be generated and considered. You want this team to help you generate ideas on how to reduce stress—you don't want the meetings to be stressful. Top management support and overall direction are important, but managers will need to give up some control in the process. Clarify that the team will not be running every idea up to the C-suite. Team members will become frustrated quickly if the CEO has to approve every suggestion they make. If there is legitimate concern about ideas that the organization simply cannot do, try to understand those limitations up front so that you can provide appropriate parameters to the team.

- If there are unions in the organization, make sure they are involved. Union participation can be tricky, particularly in facilities in which there has been infighting between unions and management. Certainly, ideas that contradict the collective bargaining agreement will be dead on arrival. Position an issue as a classic integrative bargaining situation: Addressing it helps both management and the union. Fortunately, most unions are as concerned about member stress, burnout, and turnover as you are.
- Ensure good representation from all areas of the facility. Include physicians, nurses, therapists, technicians, pharmacists, custodians, and anyone else who may be affected by stress and burnout. Also involve key external stakeholders who may play a role in potential solutions (e.g., temporary help agencies). Make sure all units are represented, because you are going to need all the help you can get to generate ideas and implement solutions. You can always break into subgroups to work on specific aspects of the project (e.g., testing an idea, collecting evaluation data). Representation does not necessarily mean that every unit, shift, or office has a person on the team. It is acceptable to have people who are responsible for representing the ideas of multiple groups. Just make sure they understand the importance of truly representing all of their areas.
- Where should you house the team? Because it will be a coalition of employees from across the organization, the team needs to avoid typical bureaucratic structures. For this reason, the team probably should not be part of the human resources (HR) department, even though much of the team's objective is HR's domain. HR is seen as answering directly to higher management, and in many organizations, the department is perceived as an administrative group with no real decision-making power. Ideally, the team's reporting structure should be outside

the organization's traditional hierarchy, like an office of clinical effectiveness (OCE) or institutional review board. Given the impact of stress and burnout on quality of care, you might consider embedding this team in your facility's OCE. The efficacy of this approach will depend on perceptions of the OCE—at some organizations, the OCE is considered an intrusive entity that dictates how work should be done. If such a perception exists, the stress management team will have difficulty gaining traction, and you might be better off setting it up as a separate department or committee even if it doesn't have a specifically designated office or staff.

Identify Challenges

My cooking and cleaning with the firefighters and sleeping in the firehouse did more than build relationships. Only through firsthand experience can one fully understand the stress when firefighters are jolted out of bed at 2:00 a.m. by a buzzer calling them out to an assignment. My involvement was a perfect opportunity to identify stressors in the firehouse.

In the same way, many of the steps you will take in building relationships also will help you identify challenges. Even when you cannot find anyone to talk to on a unit because everyone is too busy, you can glean a quick lesson from the stress they are experiencing. On the simple form in appendix B, you can record observations and compile the data you collect while building relationships and then use this information to identify challenges. Complete the form after you finish your rounds, because employees become paranoid when managers fill out forms while watching them work.

The process of identifying challenges and opportunities will be the first application of the action/reflection cycle discussed earlier. Information should be collected and integrated (with previous evidence on the topic and with the previously collected information) in a repetitive cycle.

The following paragraphs describe how that cycle might play out in an organization. Keep in mind that this approach is customizable and should be adapted as needed; the survey example may not be effective in an organization that is "surveyed out."

First, develop a list of potential challenges in the organization. Note that I use the term "challenges," not "stressors." Challenges (e.g., regulatory updates) might present difficulties in addressing stressors. These challenges need to be understood to identify opportunities later. In some cases, there may be reasons why a challenge (and subsequent stressor) exists. For example, while barcode medication administration systems add steps to the medication administration process, those additional steps enhance the safety of the system. Instead of removing those steps, staff can be trained to use the system effectively so it does not impose such a burden.

It is also important to frame the stressors as challenges. As discussed in chapter 3, stressors can be considered challenges or hindrances depending on one's perspective and the resources available to address the stressor. Framing stressors as challenges implies that they can be addressed. Stressors are often perceived as problems outside one's control. Challenges, on the other hand, are seen as tasks that can (and even must) be resolved. To be clear, don't use terms like "challenges" or, even worse, "opportunities" as euphemisms for problems. Pretending like something can be fixed when everyone knows it cannot be fixed only harms your credibility.

To identify challenges, begin with the informal observations you made while walking around your facility. From those observations, you should have an initial idea of what stressors exist in your organization. Once you have that information, work with your team to integrate it. Schedule a meeting and put the information on a whiteboard. Look for themes and don't worry if they are unrefined at the moment. The immediate goal is to form a general idea about what is happening in the organization so you know what to ask about next.

As the next step in identifying challenges and opportunities, work with your team to decide what further information you need and how you can best collect it. Don't limit your options, and don't worry about consistency across the facility. For example, you might find a quick closed-ended survey works well for physicians (open-ended questions don't work as well for them), while detailed interviews or focus groups work well with nurses. I have also found open-ended surveys are effective with pharmacists.

Further, don't limit yourself to one mode of data collection per group. After each data collection, integrate the information, determine what you have learned, and tailor the next data collection to dig deeper. For example, if your surveys indicate that people perceive a lack of management support, you could use interviews to follow up and find out more about this topic.

Joshua Baugh and his team (2021) collected data on burnout and potential contributors to burnout (e.g., workload, fairness, reward systems) in a sample of emergency physicians at an academic medical center, then fed the results back to that group in a retreat setting designed to generate ideas for how to address burnout. Collecting the survey data earlier gave their conversations during the retreat more structure and direction and provided a set of baseline data that could be useful for later evaluation of interventions.

Some data collection techniques are better suited for certain purposes. Surveys, for example, are useful for identifying stressors, determining levels of burnout, and breaking down the data by demographics (e.g., occupation, unit), but they are not well suited for identifying opportunities to reduce stress and burnout. Focus groups are good for discussing ideas, but the quantity of information you can collect will be limited because you will have to juggle the perspectives of many people at the same time, and some people may not want to share all of their ideas in public. (See appendix B for tips on running effective focus groups.) Your stress management team can coordinate these decisions so you can maximize the data you gather from each collection.

These tasks in identifying challenges and opportunities should be delegated to team members. You will find that employees are typically more comfortable talking with their peers than with a supervisor (otherwise, they would have already talked to you!). Don't take them on alone; you'll just create stress for yourself.

Identify Solutions

As you collect information about challenges and opportunities, think about (and collect information about) potential solutions. Some solutions will develop naturally. In addition to providing information about stressors, interviewees often volunteer potential fixes for the problem.

Data collection is more effective when it is structured around solutions. For focus groups in particular, ground rules should be established up front. The most important rule is to require anyone venting a concern to also offer at least one way to address it. Compliance with this rule will ensure that the focus group doesn't dissolve in a "howling session" and instead will steer the group toward coming up with challenges that have solutions.

When using interviews or focus groups to generate solutions, flesh out the participants' ideas. If someone comes up with a solution (e.g., more nurses are needed), work through how it might be implemented and any barriers that might prevent implementing the solution (e.g., availability of nurses in the local labor market). Focus groups are good for this purpose because participants can bounce ideas off each other, and you can immediately observe their reactions to those ideas.

On the downside, a focus group can get out of hand when it is running with an idea. The group may become excited about a solution and expect it to be implemented, only to become upset if it isn't. On the flip side, participants may shoot down each other's ideas prematurely and thus discourage more ideas from coming to the fore. These problems can be largely prevented by establishing clear ground rules and goals up front. Clarify that you are developing ideas that might not be implemented. Remind the group that ideas can be tested and need not be dismissed right away. You can set expectations without being negative about the process.

The person (or better, persons) running the focus group also can manage these issues. If someone consistently shoots down ideas, encourage that person to provide a solution that will work. If the group develops unrealistic expectations about implementation and immediate impact, play devil's advocate. Be careful not to take on that role too much—just enough to bring the group back to earth. Otherwise, people will start to hesitate to share ideas because they want to avoid the negative feedback.

The processes of identifying your team, challenges, and oppor-tunities will not proceed quickly—and shouldn't. Ideas need time to gel. Ideally, you should allow at least six months to build momentum, integrate ideas, and give people plenty of time to think of new solutions after the focus groups. However, do not let the processes linger indefinitely so that you lose all momentum. Once you have some initial ideas about the main challenges and opportunities in the organization, start doing something about them. Remember that generating solutions is constant. People can come up with solutions well after you have designed and imple-mented earlier ones. In fact, if a solution is working but someone proposes another that might work even better, the initiative is building upon earlier success.

Step 3: Design, Give It a Try, and Evaluate

In this step, you use the data you have collected to design interventions, test them, and evaluate their effectiveness. As in step 2, you will need to rely heavily on your team in these efforts.

Interventions do not come prepackaged. To work, they must be based on the challenges and opportunities identified in step 2. As discussed earlier, the use of individual-focused interventions has brought about the downfall of previous programs because they don't always work. BRIDGES can be tailored to help you deal with stressful situations that can lead to employee burnout at your organization. However, it is important to keep in mind that it provides a practical framework, and not an exact solution to your problems.

Consider, for example, technology. Employees feel it adds more work when it is supposed to make their lives easier. Now, suppose an employee suggests designating "super-users" of the technology to assist others. Super-users are employees with additional training in the technology who serve as go-to people for employees who work with it. Super-users are peers of those needing assistance, not information technology employees. The literature suggests that they can play an important role in shaping the attitudes and behaviors of other employees regarding new technologies (see, for example, Halbesleben et al. 2009) and that they may reduce some stress associated with implementing new technologies (see Yuan, Bradley, and Nembhard 2015).

On the basis of this idea, you could select a group of super-users, train them, and allow them to work with the technology users. Obwegeser and colleagues (2019) discuss the selection and training of super-users (not in a healthcare setting, but still applicable). They note that the intervention could last a few months or even a year. You use the tools described earlier (i.e., surveys, interviews) to review the initiative with the technology users. Based on the information that is collected, you evaluate whether the system is working and, if so, determine how it could be tweaked to work better. You might find that the super-user program is working great—no changes are needed—or that it works, but you need more super-users. Or you might find that the super-users aren't helping much because the technology is so poorly designed that even support from a super-user can't make it easier to navigate.

In this example, we have taken an idea (super-users), designed a program around it, given it a try, and evaluated it. These tasks should be repeated for every intervention you implement, no matter how big or small. Again, this step takes you through the action/reflection cycle. You try new ideas, reflect on how they worked, and then try something else.

The evaluation portion of step 3 is especially important. Too many organizational interventions are developed and implemented but not properly evaluated. Change is not the same as improvement. As a result of unforeseen circumstances, an intervention could make the situation worse. As described by Shah and colleagues (2020), electronic health records (EHRs) should improve workflows, communication, and quality of care, but instead often contribute to physician burnout because they are designed to optimize billing and similar administrative functions rather than to improve clinical decision-making. Fortunately, they offer interventions to help align EHRs with workflows by involving physicians in their implementation.

So, how do we best proceed with evaluation? Use the tools that you used to collect the data. If you conducted a survey to collect information, rerun the survey and examine how the results have changed. By using the same tool, you gather consistent measures over time.

Think carefully about the questions you are asking. Too often, organizations rely on "happy sheets" to evaluate interventions. In other words, they simply ask whether the person liked the intervention and do not consider whether it was effective. This problem has been prevalent in evaluations of crew resource management (CRM) training programs. CRM programs use aviation principles to train healthcare professionals on issues of teamwork and communication for purposes of improving patient safety. Often, however, these programs are evaluated on the basis of questions about whether the participants liked the training and whether they might use it in their jobs. Typically, they say it was great and that they will use it most of the time, but when observed later on the job, few are actually using the principles they learned. Happy-sheet evaluations only reflect a small element of an intervention's success.

To evaluate your stress management program accurately, don't just ask participants whether they liked the program. Ask whether their stress has been reduced as a result of the program (the outcome), whether they feel they are receiving more support—or whatever the target of the intervention was. These questions will prompt them to furnish the information you need to move forward.

> Evaluation is critical.
> Change is not the same as improvement.

When you have finished with step 3, you have implemented a process that will have a dramatic impact on reducing stress in your organization. The next step is to sustain the effect of this process. Chapter 6 elaborates on the final step in the program's framework— sustainability—by discussing preventive measures you can take to address long-term stress. Since sustaining your momentum is so important to this process, we will dedicate a chapter just to that aspect of the framework.

TAKEAWAY POINTS: TOOLS FOR REDUCING STRESS AND BURNOUT

This chapter covered ways to address the stress and burnout that exists in your facility. Here are three main points to take away from this chapter:

- Dealing with employees on an individual basis by enrolling them in time management programs or giving them vacation time will have little long-term value in addressing concerns with burnout in the workplace. The environmental stressors will still exist.

- Action research provides a customizable framework for addressing stress in healthcare facilities.
- The BRIDGES program framework involves a cycle of activities structured around
  - building relationships with stakeholders so they will work with you to address the stressors they face;
  - identifying a team to help you manage stress, the challenges your staff faces, and opportunities for reducing burnout;
  - designing interventions, giving them a try, and evaluating them; and
  - sustaining the change over the long term by continuing to cycle through the process.

FURTHER READING

Marquardt, M., S. Banks, P. Cauwiler, and C. S. Ng. 2018. *Optimizing the Power of Action Learning: Real-Time Strategies for Developing Leaders, Building Teams, and Transforming Organizations* (3rd ed.). New York: Mobius.

Rosa, W. E., A. E. Schlak, and C. H. Rushton. 2020. "A Blueprint for Leadership During COVID-19: Minimizing Burnout and Moral Distress Among the Nursing Workforce." *Nursing Management* 51 (8): 28–34. https://doi.org/10.1097/01 .NUMA.0000688940.29231.6f.

CHAPTER 6

Sustaining Your Momentum: Going from Burned Out to Engaged

I work here solely because of my coworkers. Without their support, I would have long since moved into a different career.

—Sonographer with 14 years of experience

If we learned anything through the pandemic, it was that we can't just throw out changes to human resource practices without considering what else needs to be in place to support those changes and what is in place that could short circuit the changes. We tried all kinds of stuff but didn't realize we were shooting ourselves in the foot because something completely different was keeping employees from using the new benefits we were offering.

—Administrator in a small rural hospital

THE GOAL OF chapter 5 was to provide you with a means of addressing the immediate symptoms of stress and burnout in your facility. It also emphasized the importance of making longer-term "lifestyle" changes in the workplace to prevent recurrences. This chapter elaborates on step 4 of the BRIDGES program framework— sustain—the component of the action research process that promotes lasting change.

Before launching into a discussion of ways to sustain your momentum to prevent stress from becoming a bigger problem, let's take a moment to frame the issue of prevention. Not every stressor in the workplace can be prevented (and shouldn't be, considering that stress in low levels generates the stimulation we need to do our jobs). My experience with a large kidney stone years ago is analogous to stress prevention. After treating it, my urologist gave me a list of steps I could take to help prevent future stones. He then informed me that even if I took all of the steps, there was still about a 50 percent chance that I would develop another stone. Nearly 15 years later, I have been able to avoid another large stone. I had to commit to following his advice and, even then, I know that getting another stone becomes more likely if I stray from that advice.

The idea is the same with stress and burnout. You can do only so much. However, if you have developed the process outlined in chapter 5 and take a few additional steps, the likelihood that stress will become a major problem will significantly decrease. And even better, taking these steps can lead to a more engaged workforce.

KEEP DOING WHAT WORKS

How can we sustain our work so that we don't run into future stress-related problems? The short answer: Close the loop. Continue to engage in walkrounds of your facility on a regular basis. Not only do walkrounds enable you to monitor stress symptoms among your staff on a continuous basis, they also are simply a good management practice.

It is important to retain your team of stress management champions. People will join and leave the team, but the basic framework should stay in place. They can continue to come up with ideas for addressing stress and can help test them. They can also help identify potential stressors in their own units and serve as critical communication channels to you. While your meetings will likely become less frequent and less intense over time, they should proceed to maintain the structure of the stress management team.

Continue to solicit ideas, give them a try, and evaluate them. Use the evaluation data from previous interventions to build on them. If something is not working, try something else based on the feedback. The idea is to build on your momentum. You may ride the momentum for a little while, but new stressors will certainly develop. If you have the basic structures outlined in this book in place, they will be easy to address before they cause burnout. If you do not and have to restart the BRIDGES program, the road to recovery from even the smallest stressors will be long.

DEVELOPMENT OF A SUPPORTIVE WORK ENVIRONMENT

One of the most important steps you can take in addressing stress long term is to develop a supportive work environment. The literature has consistently shown that social support plays a crucial role in reducing burnout. In this context, *social support* means a perception among employees that someone is on their side and willing to provide help when they need it.

Sources of Support

A few years ago, I conducted a meta-analysis of sources of social support and their relationship with burnout (see Halbesleben 2006). I wanted to determine whether some sources of support (e.g., supervisors) are more valuable than others (e.g., family, friends) in addressing burnout. My study revealed that work-related sources of support (e.g., supervisors, coworkers) had nearly *twice* as much impact in reducing burnout as nonwork sources of support. That is not to say that nonwork support isn't helpful, because support from friends and family can be helpful when you have a bad day or are swamped with work. However, if you really want to address burnout, you need to develop support networks among the people in your workplace.

Types of Support

Why are work-related sources of support so much more valuable? The answer lies in the type of support they are able to provide. Just as there are two forms of coping—active and avoidant—there are two forms of social support—instrumental and emotional. *Instrumental support* is tangible and practical. For example, if you were having a difficult time creating a chart in PowerPoint, a colleague could show instrumental support by either creating it for you or showing you how to create the chart. (The former is obviously less helpful because you will be in the same position the next time you attempt to create a chart.) *Emotional support* helps you feel better, but not necessarily by changing the situation. Again, if you were having a hard time creating a chart, your colleague would be showing emotional support if they empathized with you and said, "I feel for you. I've had that problem, too." You would take comfort in knowing that others have experienced the same problem, but emotional support won't help you much with your chart.

As you might have guessed, instrumental support reduces burnout more effectively than emotional support does. Instrumental support better addresses the underlying problem and eliminates the stressor more quickly. Again, emotional support is helpful. Knowing that someone cares for us is important to our overall well-being. Some people may be able to come up with a solution just by talking about their problem with someone, even though that person can offer only emotional support.

Keep in mind that my analysis (2006) included studies from all kinds of different industries. One could argue that emotional support, especially from coworkers, is more important in healthcare because of the very human nature of the work being done. In a systematic review of experiences of frontline healthcare professions during pandemics by Billings and colleagues (2021), researchers found that emotional support from coworkers has been especially valuable, particularly from more senior staff. Many healthcare professionals encountered emotionally difficult situations they had never encountered before and weren't trained to address.

On the same note, instrumental support may not always be the optimal solution. We all know people who are too quick to give advice, to the point where we want to avoid them even if they are often right. Moreover, as mentioned earlier, if someone else deals with the stressor (e.g., your assistant creates the PowerPoint chart for you), you will encounter the same stressor the next time around. In this way, instrumental support can enable bad behaviors. Finally, some people provide so much instrumental support to others that they have a difficult time completing their own jobs.

Thus, my meta-analysis found that work-related sources of support are more valuable than nonwork sources in dealing with burnout. Supervisors and coworkers are usually in a better position to provide the tangible, *direct,* instrumental support that is more effective in reducing burnout, whereas family and friends are in a better position to provide emotional, *indirect* support—the less valuable of the two.

There are some exceptions to this. For example, a high percentage of healthcare professionals who are partnered with other healthcare professionals could be in a great position to provide both emotional and instrumental support. Some early data coming out of the COVID-19 pandemic also suggested that family support played a larger role than previously thought in helping frontline healthcare professionals (see Giusti et al. 2020 and Karagöl and Kaya 2022 for two examples of studies on this topic).

Developing a Supportive Environment

The results of my meta-analysis suggest that to develop a supportive work environment, we need to focus on work-related sources of support and providing positive forms of instrumental support. How do we accomplish such goals?

Encouraging and rewarding supportive behavior is critical in developing a supportive environment. One of my favorite scholarly articles is titled "On the Folly of Rewarding A, While Hoping for B," by Steven Kerr (1975). It's a brilliant article about how we tend to hope something will happen, while we reward (and thus provide incentive for) the opposite. Think about supportive behavior in the context of this idea. We hope that people will help each other, but we (1) don't provide them with the time to do so, (2) don't directly reward people for helping others do their work or, even worse, (3) "punish" people for helping others—for example, we overload them with so much work that if they do help others, they won't be able to complete their own work on time. As a result, they won't bother to help anyone else.

To develop a culture of support, leaders need to make helping and teamwork organizational values. If they clearly communicate that support is a valued behavior, it will be far more likely to occur in the organization. Support can be made a valued behavior through a variety of means.

First, evaluations and rewards should be based on support. Support should be part of regular employee performance evaluations, and regular feedback should be given on supportive behaviors. If employees are reminded every few months that their support is considered an important part of their overall performance, such behaviors will become more salient. Of course, adjustments will need to be made when evaluating for helping behaviors based on the employee's level of experience.

Particularly supportive behaviors should be publicly recognized with additional rewards. These rewards don't have to be financial; simple verbal appreciation will suffice. The recognition doesn't have to come from management; peer recognition of support is far more meaningful and sets the stage for reciprocation. Giving peers an opportunity to recognize others who have helped them out in meaningful ways is a terrific way to call out the good deeds of others while demonstrating positive examples.

Second, employees need to be granted time to support each other. Lack of time is a significant barrier to engagement in supportive behaviors. Workloads should be structured such that employees can get away from their jobs long enough to help someone without negatively affecting their own performance.

One of the most important lessons from the COVID-19 pandemic and similar crises is the importance of steady, supportive, and clear communication from the highest levels of the organization. Of course, baseline information about the status of the organization and about resources the employees can use is an important starting point. However, I can't emphasize enough how important it is that your communication be regular and take on a supportive tone. Particularly in uncertain conditions where healthcare professionals face personal risks, it is valuable to remind yourself not just what information employees need, but why they need it—to help manage the fear inherent in any uncertain situation.

To that end, I implore you to ask some trusted employees, perhaps the informal leaders discussed in chapter 5, to review your communication. Too often, organizations rely on their legal counsel, human resources (HR) departments, and possibly internal strategic communication or even external crisis communication consultants to craft messages. Certainly, those stakeholders play an important role in helping you manage risk to the organization. That's their job. There may also be instances where short, cold messages to get immediate information out is necessary. But asking trusted leaders to review the content of messages ensures the tone is supportive while still delivering the necessary information.

Continuing the work started with the BRIDGES program framework intervention is certainly an important way to sustain lower levels of burnout in your organization. But recall from chapter 3 that reducing burnout is not the same as increasing engagement, despite the fact both have a foundation in similar resource processes. To truly sustain the environment that is so hard to build, we need to take a closer look at how we can go beyond just reducing burnout to providing the resources most likely to translate to employee engagement.

PUTTING IT TOGETHER: STRESS-REDUCING HUMAN RESOURCES MANAGEMENT BUNDLES AS RESOURCE CARAVANS

Tony Wheeler (2008), a researcher and dean of the college of business at Widener University, has taken the human resources management (HRM) techniques for reducing stress a step further and suggested that practices can be implemented together, or *bundled,* to create stress-reducing work environments. He based this idea on the literature on high-performance work systems, suggesting that by considering the role of stress at multiple levels of an organization's structure, we can obtain high performance through lower stress.

It's been a while since Wheeler proposed that idea, but in the intervening years, a growing body of research has backed him up. For example, a study of three Dutch organizations (one of which was a healthcare organization) found that two types of HRM bundles, maintenance bundles (which included practices like flexible work and workload management) and developmental bundles (which included practices like continuous development and participation in decision-making), were associated with higher reported resources, which were associated with higher levels of engagement (Veth et al. 2019). Similar patterns have been found in other studies across a variety of industries (Alfes et al. 2013).

If you are saying to yourself, "Wait a minute, this sounds very familiar . . .", you get bonus points for careful reading and integrating ideas. This should sound familiar because it's similar to the concept of resource caravans described in chapter 3. Putting together these HRM practices in a strategic manner helps to build up resources that work in a multiplicative fashion to support engagement.

Admittedly, the best combination of HRM practices can be tricky to identify. A close inspection of some of the literature on this topic will even reveal a very wide variety of proposed practices bundled together that can lead to some outcome. There are several instances where the specific practices in the bundles that were found to be associated with engagement may not be practical in your organization (e.g., remote work).

Similar to our approach in designing interventions, developing the specific HRM bundles will require careful thought and alignment with desired outcomes. The specific HRM practices included in HRM bundles are actually less important than the consistency with which those practices align with the goals you are trying to achieve. Consistency in alignment between HRM practices in the bundle and the goal will lead to a stronger culture around those goals, which dramatically increases the impact of the bundles on desired outcomes (Kellner et al. 2021). With that in mind, let's explore some options for types of bundles and specific HRM practices.

Stress-Reducing Bundles

Let's start with Wheeler's (2008) seminal work on this topic. He looked at traditional HRM functions such as job analysis, staffing, a multiple-hurdle selection system, formal socialization programs, performance management, job-based training, and progressive compensation systems. As noted earlier, the key to his approach is aligning those traditional HRM functions with a goal of reducing stress.

Key Components of Stress-Reducing Human Resources Management Bundles

- Comprehensive job analysis
- Appropriate staffing strategies
- Expectation management in recruitment and formal socialization programs
- Training and development opportunities
- Continuous performance management
- Progressive compensation systems

From: Wheeler 2008

Wheeler's system begins with a proper job analysis, which is the foundation of any strong HRM system. As Wheeler notes, the persistent concerns with job design in healthcare suggest that care has not been taken to analyze the requirements of the job. For example, many unintended negative consequences of technology emerge because nobody has carefully determined how the technology fits with current workflow and what knowledge or skills are required to use the technology. As I've noted elsewhere, electronic health records have typically been designed more to support billing functions than provision of care.

And as already discussed, proper registered nurse staffing ratios have a significant impact on stress and quality of care. Wheeler did not necessarily suggest that the solution is as simple as hiring more staff. The more important factor is the appropriate mix of staff. To use a sports analogy, it will do you little good if you field a baseball team with nine pitchers and no one to catch the ball.

Many organizations have addressed this problem by developing in-house flex pools or a reliance on short-term contracts with traveling staff that enable facilities to move personnel into areas that need the most staffing at a given moment. In addition to reducing stress through staff reinforcement, these pools personally benefit healthcare professionals who prefer a work schedule that is readily adjustable. Flex pools often offer options for working reduced hours or nontypical hours so professionals can maintain a balance between work and family life. Thus, such programs help full-time employees by providing backup at key times and help flex pool staff maintain their desired work–life balance. I understand that the COVID-19 pandemic exacerbated the already-massive staffing needs across healthcare professions. Fortunately, significant investments in the healthcare workforce through the 2020 Coronavirus Aid, Relief, and Economic Security (CARES) Act and the 2021 American Rescue Plan Act brought some relief in the United States. My hope is that by the time the next edition of this book is published, there will have been a significant effort to address the staffing recommendations offered by several leading advocacy groups (e.g., World Health Organization 2020) and policy researchers (e.g., Beck et al. 2021).

Unmet expectations are one of the most common instigators of burnout. This problem is a significant contributor to early-career health professional turnover, especially among nurses. The healthcare sector is seeing a great number of early-career nurses migrating to other positions or even out of the profession because the job is simply not what they had envisioned. Managing expectations is also an important element of developing engagement. It would be difficult for an employee to be engaged if they don't know what they are supposed to be engaged in. In fact, that's a big contributor to some of the issues with seemingly engaged employees crafting their jobs in unexpected directions that were mentioned in chapter 3.

To some extent, this issue needs to be addressed through education. Some schools are approaching this problem indirectly, for example, through professional development including interdisciplinary programs that work to improve communication among the various health professions. Other steps also can be taken to help align employees' expectations with emerging stressors on the job.

The first step can be taken before prospects even apply for a job. Realistic job previews (RJPs), a well-established HRM technique, provide realistic information about a position before the prospective employee even applies. The crummy working hours, difficult patients and family members, high levels of occupational injury, and so forth are all spelled out up front. In earlier iterations, RJPs were documents included with paper applications. Today, most RJPs are provided online after candidates submit their application. Some companies even have potential applicants shadow an employee for a day so they can see what working there would be like.

The evidence suggests that RJPs work. For one, they increase commitment. If an employee decides to apply for (and later take) a job even when they know it is going to be tough, they likely will be committed to it and will stick with it even through tough times. By recognizing the potential stressors of a job before taking it, employees are far less likely to experience burnout when the stressors do crop up. They will be prepared for them to happen and will have time to gather the resources necessary to meet the demands.

Healthcare organizations have been hesitant to use RJPs, probably because recruiting is so competitive that they feel they can't afford to discourage any good prospects. However, simply hiring "warm bodies" to fill positions will only cause problems down the road. If there is a poor fit between the person and the job, that person will probably become unhappy and stressed and then quit, and the position will have to be filled again. On top of that, given that burnout in organizations is emotionally contagious, that person will likely bring down the rest of the ship in the process.

Perhaps healthcare organizations hesitate to use RJPs because they don't want to hang out their dirty laundry. If they were taking the steps and measures discussed in this and the preceding chapter, however, they would have none to hang, and RJPs would just remind potential employees of stressors they already know about. Moreover, the use of RJPs might give an organization a chance to tout the many ways it is addressing those stressors. A realistic preview isn't always negative. It can describe the stressors and then follow up with steps that have been taken to address them. For example, the RJP could briefly explain the innovative scheduling systems the organization (or more accurately, its stress management team) has developed to deal with concerns over the interference of odd work schedules with family life. The RJP could even tout that the organization has a team dedicated to ensuring that stressors in the workplace are quickly addressed.

Once someone has been hired, formal socialization programs are required to manage expectations (as noted earlier) and integrate the employee into the organization's culture. The research literature suggests that socialization programs can be primary transmitters of employee culture, and programs that emphasize the organization's culture as well as networking opportunities among employees seem to improve the fit between the employee and the job more effectively than more passive forms of socialization (e.g., passing out an employee handbook or conducting a brief online training session). In turn, improved fit reduces stress and promotes engagement (Kilroy et al. 2017; Peng, Lee, and Tseng 2014). In other words, the organization's core values need to be clearly communicated to employees within their first year. These messages need to be delivered intentionally; they cannot be relayed "by accident" through passive forms of communication. Regular events should be held for new employees during their first year to help them adopt the values of the organization, including the development of a supportive environment.

One approach to cultural integration is to develop cohorts of new employees as they join the organization. Regardless of occupation or unit, they can be assigned to small groups (of about six to ten people) for informal meetings. Food is always a big draw for participation. At these meetings, you can openly discuss the organization's values. As the groups mature, you can discuss the stressors they are encountering and how they are coping with them. This discussion can support your identification processes in the BRIDGES program. This approach does two things for employees: (1) It gives them clear information about the organization's values and an opportunity to explore how their own values align with them, and (2) it gives them an opportunity to network with others from across the organization.

In addition to socialization, employees need adequate training. Education programs, even when they are based on some sort of clinical or practicum experience, cannot address all the contextual nuances of a job. Thus, while many healthcare professionals may be technically sound, they still struggle on the job because of aspects of the work or tasks specific to the workplace. Inadequate training in these areas sets them up for frustration and is a significant stressor. Think about your own position. Did you know everything about the job when you started? How long was your learning curve before you felt up to speed? (Perhaps you are still waiting for that day!) I have yet to talk with someone who was able to hit the ground running on the first day of their job because there are always things people could not know before starting.

How can we identify areas in which employees need training? A good job analysis can help with this task, as can a discussion with employees about what they wish they knew when they started. Ask them to document the knowledge, skills, and abilities (KSAs) they needed but didn't have the first day on the job. These notes can be used to develop training programs or, at the very least, be passed along to new employees so they are aware that there are KSAs that they don't yet have but will need to develop at some point.

Training is the starting point, but further professional development is important. Most healthcare professionals are intimately familiar with the grind of fulfilling continuing education requirements and do so by way of the path of least resistance. Are we really developing skills, then, or are we just checking off a chore on our to-do list? Healthcare professionals crave true development that pushes them to think and broaden their horizons, and discussion with them can elicit development opportunities. Even more gratifying for employees is to have them create new development programs for others, assuming you can grant them adequate time and support to engage in such endeavors. Employees feel empowered when they are asked to develop the skills of others. This form of development is particularly enriching in that the ultimate learner is the one doing the teaching.

Research suggests that performance feedback is an important resource that increases employee engagement (Sexton et al. 2018). Contrary to popular belief, annual performance appraisals are not effective in managing employee performance. They are a significant source of stress for all involved. Furthermore, they are often so sanitized so as not to hurt anyone's feelings that they no longer serve their original purpose (to provide meaningful feedback to employees) or their debased purpose (to document bad behavior in case someone needs to be fired). As a result, they have become almost worthless.

A better approach is to document and give regular feedback that reinforces positive behaviors regularly, not just one time per year. Problematic behavior should be documented as well, but keep in mind that, according to learning theory and research, people react better to positive reinforcement. Punishment tends to prompt avoidant behaviors, not change for the better. When emphasis is placed on what employees do wrong, they don't know what they need to do to improve. Saying "you filled that prescription incorrectly" doesn't tell people how to fill it correctly and offers little information on how to change their behavior.

The emphasis on negative behavior in performance appraisals and the avoidant behavior that results may partly explain why medical errors have become such a problem. If you knew that an error was going to appear on your next appraisal, would you report it? You might, in part because if you didn't, you could jeopardize your position, your license, and so forth. What about near misses? Information on near misses is extremely valuable but rarely reported. Exemplary organizations make a concerted effort to reward employees for reporting near misses and treat these instances as opportunities to solve a problem before it becomes a bigger problem. Such positive feedback guides people in the right direction.

An outgrowth of performance management is progressive compensation systems. To be effective, compensation systems should reflect what the organization values and reward the behavior the organization wants repeated. Effective compensation systems do so by applying a total compensation strategy that considers *all* of the ways employees are rewarded, not just their base salary (Flynn, Valentine, and Meglich 2021). Truly progressive compensation strategies also consider alignment with the values of the employee. For example, research continues to suggest generational differences in what employees value and that the most successful organizations adapt to those differences over time (Morrell and Abston 2019).

Interestingly, some forms of compensation not only reward excellent performance but also address workplace stressors. For example, a significant stressor among healthcare professionals, in part because of nonstandard working hours, is work–family conflict (Boamah and Laschinger 2016). Healthcare professionals frequently feel that their time at work is detracting from time that could be spent with family. Moreover, the strains of work can carry over to home life, and some people take out their work frustrations on their family.

Benefits that help balance work and family life can play a significant role in attracting top-quality professionals and reducing their stress. Compressed workweeks have been a common solution for many healthcare professionals. Although they make for longer working days, they are popular because they may allow for longer stretches of time to be with family or engage in other life activities (Haller et al. 2018). However, care must be taken in implementation of these programs. An influential study by Stimpfel, Sloane, and Aiken (2012) highlighted the risk of longer shifts for hospital nurses, finding that shifts over 10 hours are associated with higher burnout and lower job satisfaction. Other benefits such as childcare, eldercare, and employee assistance programs also help employees address the demands of work and family life and may offer a slight advantage in attracting healthcare professionals.

Compassionate Bundles

The HRM practices you bundle together to create resources depend entirely on the types of resources and the outcomes you are seeking to attain. Vanderbilt researcher Tim Vogus and colleagues (2021) presented compelling arguments for a "compassionate" HR bundle that would lead to collective well-being of healthcare staff while improving quality of care and efficiency. Vogus and colleagues suggested the following HRM practices:

- selection processes that screen for candidates most likely to demonstrate compassion,
- socialization of employees by consistent demonstration of compassion as a core value through everyday interactions and rituals,
- training in compassionate behaviors, and
- performance appraisals and coaching that reinforce compassion.

They also emphasized the role of standardization with customization. While these seem like competing approaches—how can you both standardize a process yet make it customized?—they can work together if managed appropriately. The goal should be standardization that allows for compassion to be offered in scale to deal with human suffering in healthcare settings. This can happen in several forms, including indirect contributors to compassion by having basic processes standardized so that healthcare providers have the time to engage in compassionate behaviors. In addition, more direct contributions to compassionate care such as standardized scripts can help providers communicate compassion to their patients and families.

Customization in this instance comes with the understanding that each patient's response to suffering is different. A hallmark of compassion is adjusting your response to how the patient is responding. As noted, standardization of processes frees up time for healthcare providers to learn more about the patient's response and possibly coordinate with others (including family) to deliver more compassionate care. Standardization with customization also may work with multiple scripts to fit the circumstances—thus, they are standardized to make it easier for the provider, but not so standard as to ignore unique patient needs. As McClelland and Vogus (2021) note, this compassionate mix allows healthcare organizations to achieve efficiency and quality in their care. And, important for our purposes, initial evidence suggests that this approach does indeed reduce burnout and provide resources that could be translated into engagement (Rathert, Ishqaidef, and Porter 2022).

Crisis Management Bundles

Drawing on lessons learned from the COVID-19 pandemic, Adikaram, Naotunna, and Priyankara (2021) proposed a combination of three HRM bundles (I'll call this a super bundle) that could help address risks such as employee health and well-being risks, financial challenges, and operational disruptions.

Their three HRM bundles correspond to each of the three risks: a health and safety bundle, a cost savings bundle, and an employee motivation and engagement bundle. The health and safety bundle involves developing procedures to address health and safety risks, clearly communicating those procedures, altering work arrangements to minimize risks, and providing the necessary support for the health and safety procedures (e.g., providing the personal protective equipment needed to follow the procedures). The cost savings bundle involves adjusting compensation to save payroll costs, managing headcount, adjusting training and development, and communicating support to employees despite the sacrifices required to reduce costs. Finally, the employee motivation and engagement bundle involves providing opportunities for engagement (primarily community-building opportunities), frequent and open communication, and providing incentives for engagement (likely redirecting funds saved from the cost savings bundle to activities more directly associated with engagement).

The work of Adikaram, Naotunna, and Priyankara is based on careful study of 26 Sri Lankan organizations, though only one was identified as a healthcare organization. As noted earlier, some specific elements of the HRM bundles may not be feasible in a healthcare setting (e.g., extensive remote work arrangements). It's also important to note that their approach is targeted for crisis management. There may be instances where their bundles compete with one another (e.g., attempting to save costs while engaging in the other bundles), particularly when one considers they were deriving their ideas from the COVID-19 pandemic. Under normal circumstances, there may be less emphasis on the cost savings or even the health and safety bundles, allowing more resources to be invested in the employee motivation and engagement bundle.

The point of this discussion is to explain the necessity of constructing an HR profile—a bundle—that not only includes many of the best HRM practices from the literature but also provides an edge in preventing stress. These bundles will sustain your BRIDGES program well into the future.

Crisis Management Human Resources Management Bundles

Health and Safety Bundle	Cost Savings Bundle	Employee Motivation and Engagement Bundle
• Implementation of health and safety measures • Communication of health and safety measures • Altered work arrangement • Health and safety support	• Compensation adjustments • Headcount management • Adjustments to training and development • Management of overhead costs • Communication of support despite changes	• Variety of opportunities for engagement • Frequent, open communication • Incentives that show support

From: Adikaram, Naotunna, and Priyankara 2021

TAKEAWAY POINTS: DEVELOPING A "STRESS-FREE ENVIRONMENT"

Implementation of the BRIDGES program described in chapter 5 is not enough to deal with stress long term. To truly reduce stress and sustain a positive environment, you will need to use some of the techniques outlined in this chapter. Because healthcare organizations traditionally have regarded the HR department not as playing a strategic role but instead fulfilling more of an administrative role, a focus on HR strategies may seem odd. Changing this perception will have a significant and positive impact on stress. The idea of HR as a department must be replaced by the idea of HR as an asset. No healthcare facility can function without the KSAs of humans, yet we do so little to develop them. The techniques suggested in this chapter will help manage healthcare professionals in a way that will also reduce stress over the long term.

Here are two main points to take away from this chapter:

- Lack of support is a major source of stress and burnout in healthcare. Development of a supportive culture will help address this problem over the long term.
- Bundles of HR practices aligned with the goals of the organization can help reduce stress. The specific practices included in these bundles may vary.

As we close out our journey toward a more engaged workforce, I want to sincerely thank you for allowing me to be part of that journey. It will require ongoing effort, but I am confident that by considering the approaches you have learned about in this book, you will be on a path toward success.

Appendix A

Resources for Dealing with Stress and Burnout

THE FOLLOWING RESOURCES supplement this text and provide relevant, interesting information about work-related stress and burnout.

WEBSITES

A variety of organizations have developed websites about work stress and burnout. Some are more work-specific and research-focused than others.

The American Psychological Association website includes a topics page about stress. Its content is general (e.g., it includes information about stress between couples in a relationship), but it provides links to many useful reports and media. It includes their large-scale assessment, "Stress in America," which provides insights regarding the experience of stress in the general population of the United States. See www.apa.org/topics/topicstress.html.

The National Institute for Occupational Safety and Health (NIOSH) has long been concerned with the impact of stress on workers' health. It has set up a site with stress resources at www.cdc.gov/niosh/topics/stress. From this website, you can access a number of stress resources, including its report *Stress . . . At Work* (www.cdc.gov/niosh/docs/99-101). The NIOSH website also includes resources about fatigue, including work schedules and their impact on stress and health. Given the significant effects that scheduling can have on healthcare professionals, you may find these resources useful. See www.cdc.gov/niosh/topics/fatigue. Last, the NIOSH website includes tools for measuring quality of work life (see www.cdc.gov/niosh/topics/stress/qwlquest.html). You may find this helpful in identifying challenges in the workplace.

The American Institute of Stress, established more than 40 years ago, provides reports that can be accessed through its website (www .stress.org); members can access additional resources such as monthly newsletters.

The National Academy of Medicine established the Action Collaborative on Clinician Well-Being and Resilience in 2019. Its website is a great resource for briefs on timely issues related to stress and well-being among clinicians. See https://nam.edu/initiatives /clinician-resilience-and-well-being/.

The American Medical Association has created a website with resources targeted at physicians. See www.ama-assn.org/amaone /equipping-physicians-manage-burnout.

Similarly, the American Nurses Association has a website with stress resources. See www.nursingworld.org/practice-policy /work-environment/health-safety/combating-stress/. The ANA also provides resources about safety at work, including issues such as needlesticks and safe patient handling. See www.nursingworld.org /practice-policy/work-environment/health-safety/safety-on-the-job/.

The American Registry for Diagnostic Medical Sonography has partnered with the APA and other groups to offer mental health resources that apply broadly to healthcare professionals. See https:// www.ardms.org/mental-health-resources/.

Certainly, there are other professional organizations that have developed resources. I encourage you to reach out to your professional organization to access them. And if they don't have resources, consider taking a leadership role in creating them!

OTHER READINGS

Books and Articles Outlining Theories Discussed in This Book

The following books and articles go into greater detail about the key theories that were used to explain stress in this book. They share the reasoning and evidence behind each theory.

Hobfoll, S. E. 1988. *The Ecology of Stress.* New York: Hemisphere.
Hobfoll, S. E., J. Halbesleben, J.-P. Neveu, and M. Westman. 2018. "Conservation of Resources in the Organizational Context: The Reality of Resources and Their Consequences." *Annual Review of Organizational Psychology and Organizational Behavior* 5: 103–28.
Lazarus, R. S., and S. Folkman. 1984. *Stress, Appraisal, and Coping.* New York: Springer.

Books and Other Resources Outlining Action Research Approaches

Although each resource takes a different approach to action research, they all follow the same basic principles of integrating employees in the process:

Clark, J. S., S. Porath, J. Thiele, and M. Jobe. 2020. *Action Research.* Manhattan, KS: New Prairie Press.
McNiff, J. 2013. *Action Research: Principles and Practice*, 3rd edition. London: Routledge.
———. 2016. *You and Your Action Research Project*, 4th edition. London: Routledge.
Stringer, E. T., and A. O. Aragón. 2020. *Action Research*, 5th edition. Thousand Oaks, CA: Sage.
Zuber-Skerritt, O. (ed.). 2021. *Action Research for Change and Development.* London: Routledge.

For those interested action research with a more academic bent, the peer-reviewed journal *Action Research* is published quarterly by Sage. See https://journals.sagepub.com/home/arj.

Other Excellent Stress-Related Books

The following books are valuable for additional depth into our understanding of stress and burnout. Admittedly, these have an academic bent. There are hundreds of other books that profess to eliminate stress with gimmicky strategies that are more likely to enrich the authors than reduce your stress.

Cooper, C. L., and J. C. Quick. 2017. *The Handbook of Stress and Health: A Guide to Research and Practice.* Hoboken, NJ: John Wiley & Sons.

Maslach, C., & Leiter, M. P. 2022. *The Burnout Challenge: Managing People's Relationships with Their Jobs.* Cambridge, MA: Harvard University Press.

OTHER LEARNING OPPORTUNITIES

Conferences and workshops are available that focus on current mechanisms for reducing stress. Now that you have some background on evidence-based approaches to stress and burnout, particularly regarding intervention, consider carefully the perspective of the workshop and the presenter. Many of these programs are not based on sound theory or science and are of little use in the long run.

That said, some good options exist. Every other year, APA and NIOSH cohost a conference on work stress and health. Information on past and future conferences is available at www.apa.org /wsh. In addition to presentations by academics conducting stress research, there are workshops on intervention techniques, "ask an expert" sessions in which you might procure advice specific to your organization, and other practical sessions. It may even be a great place to present an evaluation of your own stress reduction/prevention program based on this book. Plus, you can meet me there!

Appendix B

BRIDGES Resources

THE FOLLOWING FORMS are provided to help you organize your BRIDGES processes.

BUILDING RELATIONSHIPS FORM

The form in exhibit B.1 is designed for the relationship-building stage. It will help you (1) track the people you talk with and the areas you visit and (2) begin collecting data on existing and potential challenges.

Exhibit B.1 Building Relationships Form

Unit/department visited: _____ Date: _____ Time: _____

Whom you talked with: _____

Observations during visit (e.g., potential challenges):

Integration: How does this visit fit with others you have completed? Are any themes emerging?

Feedback provided: Based on what you observed, did you provide any feedback to the unit? Is there any remaining feedback you need to provide to the unit?

INTERVIEW FORM

The form in exhibit B.2 is only a starting point. It should be tailored to suit the needs of your organization.

Exhibit B.2: Interview Form

As you may be aware, we have created a task force dedicated to addressing stress and burnout at our facility. We are using interviews to collect information about stress from employees so we can work together to develop solutions to these issues.

1. What are the primary challenges you face in doing your job?
2. How often do you face those challenges?
3. What suggestions do you have for addressing those challenges?
4. Clarify your suggestions.
5. How would we implement them?
6. Who would be responsible for implementing them?
7. What resources would we need to implement them?
8. What do you enjoy about your job?
9. Aside from the suggestions you made in question #3, what could make your job even better?

Thank you for your candid feedback. If you have any further suggestions for our task force, please contact me at _____.

SEVEN TIPS FOR RUNNING SUCCESSFUL STRESS FOCUS GROUPS

1. Select a group that will maximize outcomes.
   a. Do not select more than 12 people. Too large a group will lead to diminishing returns.
   b. Choose people who will remain positive and provide meaningful solutions. Devil's advocates are valuable

but will need to be managed so that they do not short-circuit the group.

2. Establish rapport quickly. Introduce yourself and have the group use name tags.

3. Establish ground rules.
    a. Explain the purpose of the group (e.g., "We're seeking solutions, not just gripes.").
    b. Level the playing field. (No one's ideas are necessarily better than anyone else's.)

4. Take careful notes.
    a. Assume that notes rather than exact recordings are typically sufficient for this type of project.
    b. Work in pairs; appoint one moderator and one note taker.

5. Focus on idea development.
    a. Probe for more information if participants propose vague ideas or you need clarification. Try to do so without spending too much time on one idea unless the group sees value in fleshing out the idea.
    b. Use an idea heard earlier (e.g., in earlier focus groups) to generate discussion if the group is reluctant to talk. Develop a few ideas of your own in advance to present for feedback in case the group does not have ideas to bring to the table.

6. Facilitate more than participate.
    a. Limit your own contributions.
    b. Don't encourage one idea over another.

7. Wrap up the session and communicate next steps.
    a. Summarize the discussion.
    b. Clarify any confusion you have about the participants' suggestions.
    c. Explain the remainder of the BRIDGES program and how the task force will proceed.

References

Adikaram, A. S., N. P. G. S. I. Naotunna, and H. P. R. Priyankara. 2021. "Battling COVID-19 with Human Resource Management Bundling." *Employee Relations: The International Journal* 43 (6): 1269–89.

Alfes, K., A. D. Shantz, C. Truss, and E. C. Soane. 2013. "The Link Between Perceived Human Resource Management Practices, Engagement and Employee Behaviour: A Moderated Mediation Model." *International Journal of Human Resource Management* 24 (2): 330–51.

Ali, N. A., K. M. Wolf, J. Hammersley, S. P. Hoffmann, J. M. O'Brien Jr., G. S. Phillips, M. C. Rashkin, E. Warren, and A. Garland. 2011. "Continuity of Care in Intensive Care Units: A Cluster-Randomized Trial of Intensivist Staffing." *American Journal of Respiratory and Critical Care Medicine* 184 (7): 803–08.

American Association of Critical-Care Nurses. 2005. "AACN Standards for Establishing and Sustaining Healthy Work Environments: A Journey to Excellence." *American Journal of Critical Care* 14 (3): 187–97. https://doi.org/10.4037/ajcc2005.14.3.187.

American Institute of Stress. 2022. "Workplace Stress." Accessed June 24, 2022. www.stress.org/workplace-stress.

Arnetz, B. B., P. Lewalski, J. Arnetz, K. Breejen, and K. Przyklenk. 2017. "Examining Self-Reported and Biological Stress and Near Misses Among Emergency Medicine Residents: A Single-Centre Cross-Sectional Assessment in the USA." *BMJ Open* 7 (8): e016479. https://doi.org/10.1136/bmjopen-2017-016479.

Bailey, C., A. Madden, K. Alfes, and L. Fletcher. 2017. "The Meaning, Antecedents and Outcomes of Employee Engagement: A Narrative Synthesis." *International Journal of Management Reviews* 19 (1): 31–53. https://doi.org/10.1111/ijmr.12077.

Barrett, A. 2020. "'I Can Tell You Right Now, EHR Does Not Improve Communication. It Does Not Improve Healthcare': Understanding How Providers Make Sense of Advanced Information Technology Workarounds." *Journal of Applied Communication Research* 48 (5): 537–57. https://doi.org/10.1080/00909882.2020.1820551.

Baugh, J. J., A. S. Raja, and J. K. Takayesu. 2021. "Help Us Help You: Engaging Emergency Physicians to Identify Organizational Strategies to Reduce Burnout." *Western Journal of Emergency Medicine* 22 (3): 696–701. https://doi.org/10.5811/westjem.2020.49180.

Beck, A. J., J. Spetz, P. Pittman, B. K. Frogner, E. P. Fraher, J. Moore, D. Armstrong, and P. I. Buerhaus. 2021. "Investing in a 21st Century Health Workforce: A Call for Accountability." *Health Affairs,* September 25. www.healthaffairs.org/do/10.1377/forefront.20210913.133585.

Billings, J., B. C. F. Ching, V. Gkofa, T. Greene, and M. Bloomfield. 2021. "Experiences of Frontline Healthcare Workers and Their Views About Support During COVID-19 and Previous Pandemics: A Systematic Review and Qualitative Meta-Synthesis." *BMC Health Services Research.* 21 (1): 1–17. https://doi.org/10.1186/s12913-021-06917-z.

Boamah, S. A., and H. Laschinger. 2016. "The Influence of Areas of Work–Life Fit and Work–Life Interference on Burnout and Turnover Intentions Among New Graduate Nurses." *Journal of Nursing Management* 24 (2): e164–74. https://doi.org/10.1111/jonm.12318.

Brazier, A., E. Larson, Y. Xu, G. Judah, M. Egan, H. Burd, and A. Darzi. 2022. "'Dear Doctor': A Randomised Controlled Trial of a Text Message Intervention to Reduce Burnout in Trainee Anaesthetists." *Anaesthesia* 77 (4): 405–15. https://doi.org/10.1111/anae.15643.

Britt, T. W., C. A. Castro, and A. B. Adler. 2005. "Self-Engagement, Stressors, and Health: A Longitudinal Study." *Personality and Social Psychology Bulletin* 31: 1475–86. https://doi.org/10.1177/0146167205276525.

Carmona-Halty, M. A., W. B. Schaufeli, and M. Salanova. 2019. "The Utrecht Work Engagement Scale for Students (UWES–9S): Factorial Validity, Reliability, and Measurement Invariance in a Chilean Sample of Undergraduate University Students." *Frontiers in Psychology* 10, https://doi.org/10.3389/fpsyg.2019.01017.

Cimiotti, J. P., L. H. Aiken, D. M. Sloane, and E. S. Wu. 2012. "Nurse Staffing, Burnout, and Health Care-Associated Infection." *American Journal of Infection Control* 40 (6): 486–90. https://doi.org/10.1016/j.ajic.2012.02.029.

Cohen, S., T. Kamarck, and R. Mermelstein. 1983. "A Global Measure of Perceived Stress." *Journal of Health and Social Behavior* 24 (4): 385–96.

Colindres, C. V., E. Bryce, P. Coral-Rosero, R. M. Ramos-Soto, F. Bonilla, and A. Yassi. 2018. "Effect of Effort–Reward Imbalance and Burnout on Infection Control Among Ecuadorian Nurses." *International Nursing Review* 65 (2): 190–99. https://doi.org/10.1111/inr.12409.

Cooper-Thomas, H. D., J. Xu, and A. M. Saks. 2018. "The Differential Value of Resources in Predicting Employee Engagement." *Journal of Managerial Psychology* 33 (4/5): 32644. https://doi.org/10.1108/JMP-12-2017-0449.

Crawford, E. R., J. A. LePine, and B. L. Rich. 2010. "Linking Job Demands and Resources to Employee Engagement and Burnout: A Theoretical Extension and Meta-Analytic Test." *Journal of Applied Psychology* 95 (5): 834. https://doi.org/10.1037/a0019364.

Crawford, E. R., B. L. Rich, B. Buckman, and J. Bergeron. 2013. "The Antecedents and Drivers of Employee Engagement." In *Employee Engagement in Theory and Practice*, edited by C. Truss, K. Alfes, R. Delbridge, A. Shantz, and E. Soane, 71–95. London: Routledge.

Dall'Ora, C., J. Ball, M. Reinius, and P. Griffiths. 2020. "Burnout in Nursing: A Theoretical Review." *Human Resources for Health* 18 (1): 1–17. https://doi.org/10.1186/s12960-020-00469-9.

de Lima Garcia, C., I. Bezerra, J. Ramos, J. do Valle, M. L. Bezerra de Oliveira, and L. C. Abreu. 2019. "Association Between Culture of Patient Safety and Burnout in Pediatric Hospitals." *PLoS ONE* 14 (6): e0218756. https://doi.org/10.1371/journal .pone.0218756.

Demerouti, E., A. B. Bakker, I. Vardakou, and A. Kantas. 2002. "The Convergent Validity of Two Burnout Instruments: A Multitrait-Multimethod Analysis." *European Journal of Psychological Assessment* 18: 296–307.

Demichelis, O. P., S. A. Grainger, K. T. McKay, X. E. Bourda- niotis, E. G. Churchill, and J. D. Henry. 2022. "Sleep, Stress and Aggression: Meta-Analyses Investigating Associations and Causality." *Neuroscience & Biobehavioral Reviews* 139: 104732. https://doi.org/10.1016/j.neubiorev.2022.104732.

Downey, M., S. Parslow, and M. Smart. 2011. "The Hidden Treasure in Nursing Leadership: Informal Leaders." *Journal of Nursing Management* 19 (4): 517–21. https://doi .org/10.1111/j.1365-2834.2011.01253.x.

Dunn, P. M., B. B. Arnetz, J. F. Christensen, and L. Homer. 2007. "Meeting the Imperative to Improve Physician Well-Being: Assessment of an Innovative Program." *Journal of General Internal Medicine* 22 (11): 1544–52. https://doi.org/10.1007 /s11606-007-0363-5.

Dyrbye, L. N., D. Major-Elechi, J. T. Hays, C. H. Fraser, S. J. Buskirk, and C. P. West. 2020. "Relationship Between Orga- nizational Leadership and Health Care Employee Burnout and Satisfaction." *Mayo Clinic Proceedings* 95 (4): 698–708.

Flynn, W. J., S. R. Valentine, and P. Meglich. 2021. *Healthcare Human Resource Management.* Boston: Cengage Learning.

French, S. E., R. Lenton, V. Walters, and J. Eyles. 2000. "An Empiri- cal Evaluation of the Expanded Nursing Stress Scale." *Journal of Nursing Measurement* 8 (2): 161–78.

Galanis, P., I. Vraka, D. Fragkou, A. Bilali, and D. Kaitelidou. 2021. "Nurses' Burnout and Associated Risk Factors During the COVID-19 Pandemic: A Systematic Review and Meta-Analysis." *Journal of Advanced Nursing* 77 (8): 3286–302. https://doi.org/10.1111/jan.14839.

Gallup Organization. 1992. *Gallup Workplace Audit.*

Gawke, J. C., M. J. Gorgievski, and A. B. Bakker. 2017. "Employee Intrapreneurship and Work Engagement: A Latent Change Score Approach." *Journal of Vocational Behavior* 100: 88–100. https://doi.org/10.1016/j.jvb.2017.03.002.

Gintoli, I., E. Boietti, F. Bert, S. Barbaro, D. Corsi, D. Griffa, G. Rabacchi, A. Scarmozzino, and R. Siliquini. 2021. "Is the Hospital Safety Walkround Effective to Control the Risk of Contagion During COVID-19 Pandemic?" *European Journal of Public Health* 31 (Supplement 3): 165–484. https://doi.org/10.1093/eurpub/ckab165.484.

Giusti, E. M., E. Pedroli, G. E. D'Aniello, C. Stramba Badiale, G. Pietrabissa, C. Manna, M. Stramba Badiale, G. Riva, G. Castelnuovo, and E. Molinari. 2020. "The Psychological Impact of the COVID-19 Outbreak on Health Professionals: A Cross-Sectional Study. *Frontiers in Psychology* 11: 1684. https://doi.org/10.3389/fpsyg.2020.01684.

Gray-Toft, P., and J. G. Anderson. 1981. "The Nursing Stress Scale: Development of an Instrument." *Journal of Behavioral Assessment* 3 (1): 11–23.

Hafner, M., M. Stepanek, E. Iakovidou, and C. Van Stolk. 2020. "Employee Engagement in the NHS: A Secondary Data Analysis of the NHS Healthy Workforce and Britain's Healthiest Workplace Surveys." *RAND Health Quarterly* 9 (1): 3.

Halbesleben, J. R. B. 2006. "Sources of Social Support and Burnout: A Meta-Analytic Test of the Conservation of Resources Model." *Journal of Applied Psychology* 91 (5): 1134–45. https://doi.org/10.1037/0021-9010.91.5.1134.

Halbesleben, J. R. B. 2021. "Individual-Level Outcomes of Employee Engagement: A Conservation of Resources Framework." In *A*

Research Agenda for Employee Engagement in a Changing World of Work, edited by J. P. Meyer and B. Schneider, 87–100. Northampton, MA: Edward Elgar Publishing.

Halbesleben, J. R. B., J. Harvey, and M. C. Bolino. 2009. "Too Engaged? A Conservation of Resources View of the Relationship Between Work Engagement and Work Interference with Family." *Journal of Applied Psychology* 94 (6): 1452–65.

Halbesleben, J. R. B., H. K. Osburn, and M. D. Mumford. 2006. "Action Research as a Burnout Intervention: Reducing Burnout in the Federal Fire Service." *Journal of Applied Behavioral Science* 42 (2): 244–66. https://doi.org/10.1177/0021886305285031.

Halbesleben, J. R. B., C. Rathert, and E. S. Williams. 2013. "Emotional Exhaustion and Medication Administration Work-Arounds: The Moderating Role of Nurse Satisfaction with Medication Administration." *Health Care Management Review* 38 (2): 95–104. https://doi.org/10.1097/HMR.0b013e3182452c7f.

Halbesleben, J. R. B., B. J. Wakefield, D. S. Wakefield, and L. Cooper. 2008. "Nurse Burnout and Patient Safety Outcomes: Nurse Safety Perception vs. Reporting Behavior." *Western Journal of Nursing Research* 30 (5): 560–77. https://doi.org/10.1177/0193945907311322.

Halbesleben, J. R. B., D. S. Wakefield, M. M. Ward, J. Brokel, and D. Crandall. 2009. "The Relationship Between Super Users' Attitudes and Employee Experiences with Clinical Information Systems." *Medical Care Research and Review* 66 (1): 82–96. https://doi.org/10.1177/1077558708325984.

Hall, L. H., J. Johnson, I. Watt, and D. B. O'Connor. 2019. "Association of GP Wellbeing and Burnout with Patient Safety in UK Primary Care: A Cross-Sectional Survey." *British Journal of General Practice* 69 (684): e507–14. https://doi.org/10.3399/bjgp19X702713.

Haller, T., B. A. Quatrara, L. C. Letzkus, and J. Keim-Malpass. 2018. "Nurses' Perceptions of Shift Length: What Are the Benefits?" *Nursing Management* 49 (10): 38–43. https://doi.org/10.1097/01.NUMA.0000546202.40080.cl.

Hambrick, E. P., T. W. Brawner, and B. D. Perry. 2019. "Timing of Early-Life Stress and the Development of Brain-Related Capacities." *Frontiers in Behavioral Neuroscience* 13. https://doi.org/10.3389/fnbeh.2019.00183.

Harter, J. K., F. L. Schmidt, J. W. Asplund, E. A. Killham, and S. Agrawal, 2010. "Causal Impact of Employee Work Perceptions on the Bottom Line of Organizations." *Perspectives on Psychological Science* 5: 378–89. https://doi.org/10.1177/1745691610374589.

Hickey, B. A., T. Chalmers, P. Newton, C.-T. Lin, D. Sibbritt, C. S. McLachlan, R. Clifton-Bligh, J. Morley, and S. Lal. 2021. "Smart Devices and Wearable Technologies to Detect and Monitor Mental Health Conditions and Stress: A Systematic Review." *Sensors* 21 (10): 3461. https://doi.org/10.3390/s21103461.

Higgins, C., L. Duxbury, and S. Lyons. 2008. "Reducing Work–Life Conflict. What Works? What Doesn't?" Accessed June 24, 2022. www.canada.ca/en/health-canada/services/environmental-workplace-health/reports-publications/occupational-health-safety/reducing-work-life-conflict-what-works-what-doesn.html.

Hobfoll, S. E. 2011. "Conservation of Resource Caravans and Engaged Settings." *Journal of Occupational and Organizational Psychology* 84 (1): 116–22.

Hobfoll, S. E. 1988. *The Ecology of Stress.* New York: Hemisphere.

Holmes, T. H., and R. H. Rahe. 1967. "The Social Readjustment Rating Scale." *Journal of Psychosomatic Research* 11 (2): 213–18.

Jackson, J. S., K. M. Knight, and J. A. Rafferty. 2010. "Race and Unhealthy Behaviors: Chronic Stress, the HPA Axis, and Physical and Mental Health Disparities Over the Life Course." *American Journal of Public Health* 100: 933–39.

Jones, J. W. 1980. *Preliminary Manual: The Staff Burnout Scale for Health Professionals.* Park Ridge, IL: London House.

Jun, J., M. M. Ojemeni, R. Kalamani, J. Tong, and M. L. Crecelius. 2021. "Relationship Between Nurse Burnout, Patient and Organizational Outcomes: Systematic Review." *International Journal of Nursing Studies* 119. https://doi.org/10.1016/j.ijnurstu.2021.103933.

Kahn, W. 1990. "Psychological Conditions of Personal Engagement and Disengagement at Work." *Academy of Management Journal* 33: 692–724.

Kalmoe, M. C., M. B. Chapman, J. A. Gold, and A. M. Giedinghagen. 2019. "Physician Suicide: A Call to Action." *Missouri Medicine* 116 (3): 211–16. https://pubmed.ncbi.nlm.nih.gov/31527944/.

Karagöl, A., and Z. T. Kaya. 2022. "Healthcare Workers' Burn-out, Hopelessness, Fear of COVID-19 and Perceived Social Support Levels." *European Journal of Psychiatry*. January. https://doi.org/10.1016/j.ejpsy.2022.01.001.

Kellner, A., K. Townsend, R. Loudoun, and A. Wilkinson. 2021. "High Reliability Human Resource Management (HRM): A System for High Risk Workplaces." *Human Resource Management Journal*. https://doi.org/10.1111/1748-8583.12424.

Kelly, R. J., and L. R. Hearld. 2020. "Burnout and Leadership Style in Behavioral Health Care: A Literature Review." *Journal of Behavioral Health Services & Research* 47 (4): 581–600. https://doi.org/10.1007/s11414-019-09679-z.

Kerr, S. 1975. "On the Folly of Rewarding A, While Hoping for B." *Academy of Management Journal* 18: 769–783. https://doi.org/10.5465/255378.

Keyko, K., G. G. Cummings, O. Yonge, and C. A. Wong. 2016. "Work Engagement in Professional Nursing Practice: A Systematic Review." *International Journal of Nursing Studies* 61: 142–64. https://doi.org/10.1016/j.ijnurstu.2016.06.003.

Kilroy, S., P. C. Flood, J. Bosak, and D. Chênevert. 2017. "Perceptions of High-Involvement Work Practices, Person–Organization Fit, and Burnout: A Time-Lagged Study of Health Care Employees." *Human Resource Management* 56 (5): 821–83. https://doi.org/10.1002/HRM.21803.

Koranne, R., E. S. Williams, S. Poplau, K. M. Banks, M. Sonneborn, H. R. Britt, and M. Linzer. 2022. "Reducing Burnout and Enhancing Work Engagement Among Clinicians: The Minnesota Experience." *Health Care Management Review* 47 (1): 49–57. https://doi.org/10.1097/HMR.0000000000000298.

Kristensen, T. S., M. Borritz, E. Villadsen, and K. B. Christensen. 2005. "The Copenhagen Burnout Inventory: A New Tool for the Assessment of Burnout." *Work and Stress* 19 (3): 192–207. https://doi.org/10.1080/02678370500297720.

Kwon, K-B., and T. Kim. 2020. "An Integrative Literature Review of Employee Engagement and Innovative Behavior: Revisiting The JD-R Model." *Human Resource Management Review* 30 (2): 100704. https://doi.org/10.1016/J.HRMR.2019.100704.

Laschinger, H. K. S., L. Borgogni, C. Consiglio, and E. Read. 2015. "The Effects of Authentic Leadership, Six Areas of Worklife, and Occupational Coping Self-Efficacy on New Graduate Nurses' Burnout and Mental Health: A Cross-Sectional Study." *International Journal of Nursing Studies* 52 (6): 1080–89. https://doi.org/10.1016/j.ijnurstu.2015.03.002.

Laschinger, H. K. S., and E. A. Read. 2016. "The Effect of Authentic Leadership, Person–Job Fit, and Civility Norms on New Graduate Nurses' Experiences of Coworker Incivility and Burnout." *Journal of Nursing Administration* 46 (11): 574–80. https://doi.org/10.1097/NNA.0000000000000407.

Lazarus, R. S., and S. Folkman. 1984. *Stress, Appraisal, and Coping.* New York: Springer.

Ma, Y., N. A. Faraz, F. Ahmed, M. K. Iqbal, U. Saeed, M. F. Mughal, and A. Raza. 2021. "Curbing Nurses' Burnout During COVID-19: The Roles of Servant Leadership and Psychological Safety." *Journal of Nursing Management* 29 (8): 2383–91. https://doi.org/10.1111/jonm.13414.

MacLeod, D., and N. Clarke. 2009. "Engaging for Success: Enhancing Performance Through Employee Engagement" (report to government). Accessed June 24, 2022. http://www.allthingsic.com/wp-content/uploads/2011/10/TheMacleodReport.pdf.

Mandeville, A., J. Halbesleben, and M. Whitman. 2016. "Misalignment and Misperception in Preferences to Utilize Family-Friendly Benefits: Implications for Benefit Utilization and Work–Family Conflict." *Personnel Psychology* 69 (4): 895–929. https://doi.org/10.1111/PEPS.12124.

Maslach, C. 1982. *Burnout: The Cost of Caring.* Englewood Cliffs, NJ: Prentice Hall.

Maslach, C., and S. Jackson. 1981. "The Measurement of Experienced Burnout." *Journal of Occupational Behavior* 2: 99–113.

Matthews, R. A., M. J. Mills, and S. Wise. 2020. "Advancing Research and Practice Through an Empirically Validated Short-Form Measure of Work Engagement." *Occupational Health Science* 4 (3): 305–31. https://doi.org/10.1007/s41542-020-00071-4.

McClelland, L. E., and T. J. Vogus. 2021. "Infusing, Sustaining, and Replenishing Compassion in Health Care Organizations Through Compassion Practices." *Health Care Management Review* 46 (1): 55–65. https://doi.org/10.1007/s41542-020-00071-4.

Montgomery, A. P., A. Azuero, M. Baernholdt, L. A. Loan, R. S. Miltner, H. Qu, D. Raju, and P. A. Patrician. 2021. "Nurse Burnout Predicts Self-Reported Medication Administration Errors in Acute Care Hospitals." *Journal for Healthcare Quality* 43 (1): 13–23. https://doi.org/10.1097/JHQ.0000000000000274.

Moriates, C., E. Schulwolf, F. P. Hudson, K. Nieto, L. Miller, M. Pignone, and R. Pierce. 2022. "A Different Kind of Leadership Rounds System Thinking to the Bedside and Bedside to Systems Thinkers." Accessed June 24, 2022. www.the-hospitalist.org/hospitalist/article/31432/hospital-medicine/a-different-kind-of-leadership-rounds/.

Morrell, D. L., and K. A. Abston. 2018. "Millennial Motivation Issues Related to Compensation and Benefits: Suggestions for Improved Retention." *Compensation & Benefits Review* 50 (2): 107–13. https://doi.org/10.1177/0886368718822053.

National Institute for Occupational Safety and Health (NIOSH). 1999. "Stress . . . At Work." Accessed June 24, 2022. www.cdc.gov/niosh/docs/99-101.

Neuber, L., C. Englitz, N. Schulte, B. Forthmann, and H. Holling. 2022. "How Work Engagement Relates to Performance and Absenteeism: A Meta-Analysis." *European Journal of Work and Organizational Psychology* 31 (2): 292–315. https://doi.org/10.1080/1359432X.2021.1953989.

Nursing Solutions, Inc. 2022. "2022 National Healthcare Retention & RN Staffing Report." Accessed June 6, 2022. www.nsi nursingsolutions.com/Documents/Library/NSI_National_ Health_Care_Retention_Report.pdf.

Obwegeser, N., P. Danielsen, K. Sandfeld Hansen, M. A. Helt, and L. H. Nielsen. 2019. "Selection and Training of Super-Users for ERP Implementation Projects." *Journal of Information Technology Case and Application Research* 21 (2): 74–89. https://doi.org/10 .1080/15228053.2019.1631606.

Panagioti, M., E. Panagopoulou, P. Bower, G. Lewith, E. Kontopantelis, C. Chew-Graham, S. Dawson, H. van Marwijk, K. Geraghty, and A. Esmail. 2017. "Controlled Interventions to Reduce Burnout in Physicians: A Systematic Review and Meta-Analysis." *JAMA Internal Medicine* 177 (2): 195–205. https:// doi.org/10.1001/jamainternmed.2016.7674.

Peng, J-C., Y-L. Lee, and M-M. Tseng. 2014. "Person–Organization Fit and Turnover Intention: Exploring the Mediating Effect of Work Engagement and the Moderating Effect of Demand–Ability Fit." *Journal of Nursing Research* 22 (1): 1–11. https://doi .org/10.1097/jnr.0000000000000019.

Poulsen, A. A., P. Meredith, A. Khan, J. Henderson, V. Castrisos, and S. R. Khan. 2014. "Burnout and Work Engagement in Occupational Therapists." *British Journal of Occupational Therapy* 77 (3): 156–64. https://doi.org/10.4276/0308022 14X13941036266621.

Prapanjaroensin, A., P. A. Patrician, and D. E. Vance. 2017. "Conservation of Resources Theory in Nurse Burnout and Patient Safety." *Journal of Advanced Nursing* 73 (11): 2558–65. https:// doi.org/10.1111/jan.13348.

Prins, J. T., F. M. M. A. Van Der Heijden, J. E. H. M. Hoekstra-Weebers, A. B. Bakker, H. B. M. van de Wiel, B. Jacobs, and S. M. Gazendam-Donofrio. 2009. "Burnout, Engagement and Resident Physicians' Self-Reported Errors." *Psychology, Health & Medicine* 14 (6): 654–66. https://doi.org/10.1080/13548500 903311554.

Rathert, C., G. Ishqaidef, and T. H. Porter. 2022. "Caring Work Environments and Clinician Emotional Exhaustion: Empirical Test of an Exploratory Model." *Health Care Management Review* 47 (1): 58–65. https://doi.org/1097/HMR.0000000000000294.

Rathert, C., E. S. Williams, E. R. Lawrence, and J. R. B. Halbesleben. 2012. "Emotional Exhaustion and Workarounds in Acute Care: Cross Sectional Tests of a Theoretical Framework." *International Journal of Nursing Studies.* 49 (8): 969–77. https://doi.org/10.1016/j.ijnurstu.2012.02.011.

Reid, R. J., K. Coleman, E. A. Johnson, P. A. Fishman, C. Hsu, M. P. Soman, C. E. Trescott, M. Erikson, and E. B. Larson. 2010. "The Group Health Medical Home at Year Two: Cost Savings, Higher Patient Satisfaction, and Less Burnout for Providers." *Health Affairs* 29 (5): 835–43. https://doi.org/10.1377/hlthaff.2010.0158.

Rich, B. L., J. A. Lepine, and E. R. Crawford. 2010. "Job Engagement: Antecedents and Effects on Job Performance." *Academy of Management Journal* 53 (3): 617–35. https://doi.org/10.5465/amj.2010.51468988.

Saks, A. M. 2006. "Antecedents and Consequences of Employee Engagement." *Journal of Managerial Psychology* 21 (7): 600–19. https://doi.org/10.1108/02683940610690169.

Saks, A. M., and J. A. Gruman. 2014. "What Do We Really Know About Employee Engagement?" *Human Resource Development Quarterly* 25 (2): 155–82. https://doi.org/10.1002/hrdq.21187.

Salyers, M. P., K. A. Bonfils, L. Luther, R. L. Firmin, D. A. White, E. L. Adams, and A. L. Rollins. 2017. "The Relationship Between Professional Burnout and Quality and Safety in Healthcare: A Meta-Analysis." *Journal of General Internal Medicine* 32 (4): 475–82. https://doi.org/10.1007/s11606-016-3886-9.

Schaufeli, W. B., A. B. Bakker, and M. Salanova. 2006. "The Measurement of Work Engagement with a Short Questionnaire: A Cross-National Study." *Educational and Psychological Measurement* 66 (4): 701–16. https://doi.org/10.1177/0013164405282471.

Schaufeli, W. B., M. Salanova, V. González-Romá, and A. B. Bakker. 2002. "The Measurement of Engagement and Burnout: A Confirmative Analytic Approach." *Journal of Happiness Studies* 3: 71–92.

Sexton, J. B., K. C. Adair, M. W. Leonard, T. C. Frankel, J. Proulx, S. R. Watson, B. Magnus, B. Bogan, M. Jamal, R. Schwendimann, and A. S. Frankel. 2018. "Providing Feedback Following Leadership WalkRounds is Associated with Better Patient Safety Culture, Higher Employee Engagement and Lower Burnout." *BMJ Quality & Safety* 27 (4): 261–70. http://dx.doi.org/10.1136/bmjqs-2016-006399.

Sexton, J. B., K. C. Adair, J. Profit, J. Bae, K. J. Rehder, T. Gosselin, J. Milne, M. Leonard, and A. Frankel. 2021. "Safety Culture and Workforce Well-Being Associations with Positive Leadership WalkRounds." *The Joint Commission Journal on Quality and Patient Safety* 47 (7): 403–11. https://doi.org/10.1016/j.jcjq.2021.04.001.

Shah, M. K., D. Gandrakota, J. P. Cimiotti, N. Ghose, M. Moore, and M. K. Ali. 2021. "Prevalence of and Factors Associated with Nurse Burnout in the US." *JAMA Network Open* 4 (2). https://doi.org/1010.1001/jamanetworkopen.2020.36469.

Shah, T., A. B. Kitts, J. A. Gold, K. Horvath, A. Ommaya, F. Opelka, L. Sato, G. Schwarze, M. Upton, and L. Sandy. 2020. EHR Optimization and Clinician Well-Being: A Potential Roadmap Toward Action. *NAM Perspectives* (discussion paper), National Academy of Medicine, Washington, DC. https://doi.org/10.31478/202008a.

Shanafelt, T. D., G. Gorringe, R. Menaker, K. A. Storz, D. Reeves, S. J. Buskirk, J. A. Sloan, and S. J. Swensen. 2015. "Impact of Organizational Leadership on Physician Burnout and Satisfaction." *Mayo Clinic Proceedings* 90 (4): 432–40. https://doi.org/10.1016/j.mayocp.2015.01.012.

Shirom, A. 2008. *Shirom-Melamed Vigor Measure (SMVM)* (database record), APA PsycTests. https://doi.org/10.1037/t32874-000.

Shoureshi, P., M. Guerre, C. A. Seideman, D. G. Callejas, C. L. Amling, S. Bassale, and J. D. Chouhan. 2022. "Addressing Burnout in Urology: A Qualitative Assessment of Interventions." *Urology Practice* 9 (1): 101–07. https://doi.org/10.1097/UPJ.0000000000000282.

Sinclair, S., S. Raffin-Bouchal, L. Venturato, J. Mijovic-Kondejewski, and L. Smith-MacDonald. 2017. "Compassion Fatigue: A Meta-Narrative Review of the Healthcare Literature." *International Journal of Nursing Studies.* 69 (1): 9–24. https://doi.org/10.1016/j.ijnurstu.2017.01.003.

Sinsky, C. A., L. D. Biddison, A. Mallick, A. Legreid Dopp, J. Perlo, L. Lynn, and C. D. Smith. 2020. "Organizational Evidence-Based and Promising Practices for Improving Clinician Well-Being." *NAM Perspectives.* Discussion paper, National Academy of Medicine, Washington, DC. https://doi.org/10.31478/202011a.

Soane, E., C. Truss, K. Alfes, A. Shantz, C. Rees, and M. Gatenby. 2012. "Development and Application of a New Measure of Employee Engagement: The ISA Engagement Scale." *Human Resource Development International* 15 (5): 529–47. https://doi.org/10.1080/13678868.2012.726542.

Stimpfel, A. W., D. M. Sloane, and L. H. Aiken. 2012. "The Longer the Shifts for Hospital Nurses, the Higher the Levels of Burnout and Patient Dissatisfaction." *Health Affairs* 31 (11): 2501–09. https://doi.org/10.1377/hlthaff.2011.1377.

Swensen, S., A. Kabcenell, and T. Shanafelt. 2016. "Physician–Organization Collaboration Reduces Physician Burnout and Promotes Engagement: The Mayo Clinic Experience." *Journal of Healthcare Management* 61 (2): 105–27.

Tawfik, D. S., J. Profit, T. I. Morgenthaler, D. V. Satele, C. A. Sinsky, L. N. Dyrbye, M. A. Tutty, C. P. West, and T. D. Shanafelt. 2018. "Physician Burnout, Well-Being, and Work Unit Safety Grades in Relationship to Reported Medical Errors." *Mayo Clinic Proceedings* 93 (11): 1571–80. https://doi.org/10.1016/j.mayocp.2018.05.014.

Trougakos, J. P., I. Hideg, B. H. Cheng, and D. J. Beal. 2014. "Lunch Breaks Unpacked: The Role of Autonomy as a Moderator of Recovery During Lunch." *Academy of Management Journal* 57 (2): 405–21. https://doi.org/10.5465/amj.2011.1072.

Van Bogaert, P., L. Peremans, D. Van Heusden, M. Verspuy, V. Kureckova, Z. Van de Cruys, and E. Franck. 2017. "Predictors of Burnout, Work Engagement and Nurse Reported Job Outcomes and Quality of Care: A Mixed Method Study." *BMC Nursing* 16 (1): 1–14. https://doi.org/10.1186/s12912-016-0200-4.

Veth, K. N., H. P. L. M. Korzilius, B. I. J. M. Van der Heijden, B. J. M. Emans, and A. H. De Lange. 2019. "Understanding the Contribution of HRM Bundles for Employee Outcomes Across the Life-Span." *Frontiers in Psychology*. https://doi.org/10: 2518. 10.3389/fpsyg.2019.02518.

Vogus, T. J., L. E. McClelland, Y. S. H. Lee, K. L. McFadden, and X. Hu. 2021. "Creating a Compassion System to Achieve Efficiency and Quality in Health Care Delivery." *Journal of Service Management* 32 (4): 560–80. https://doi.org/10.1108/JOSM-05-2019-0132.

Wake, M., and W. Green. 2019. "Relationship Between Employee Engagement Scores and Service Quality Ratings: Analysis of the National Health Service Staff Survey Across 97 Acute NHS Trusts in England and Concurrent Care Quality Commission Outcomes (2012–2016)." *BMJ Open* 9 (7): e026472. https://doi.org/10.1136/bmjopen-2018-026472.

Ward, M. E., A. De Brún, D. Beirne, C. Conway, U. Cunningham, A. English, J. Fitzsimons, E. Furlong, Y. Kane, A. Kelly, S. McDonnell, S. McGinley, B. Monaghan, A. Myler, E. Nolan, R. O'Donovan, M. O'Shea, A. Shuhaiber, and E. McAuliffe. 2018. "Using Co-Design to Develop a Collective Leadership Intervention for Healthcare Teams to Improve Safety Culture." *International Journal of Environmental Research and Public Health* 15 (6): e1182. https://doi.org/10.3390/ijerph15061182.

Wee, K. Z., and A. Y. Lai. 2022. "Work Engagement and Patient Quality of Care: A Meta-Analysis and Systematic Review."

Medical Care Research and Review 79 (3): 345–58. https://doi .org/10.1177/10775587211030388.

Wei, H., A. King, Y. Jiang, K. A. Sewell, and D. M. Lake. 2020. "The Impact of Nurse Leadership Styles on Nurse Burnout: A Systematic Literature Review." *Nurse Leader* 18 (5): 439–50. https://doi.org/10.1016/j.mnl.2020.04.002.

West, C. P., N. Liselotte, P. J. E. Dyrbye, and T. D. Shanafelt. 2016. "Interventions to Prevent and Reduce Physician Burnout: A Systematic Review and Meta-Analysis." *Lancet* 388 (10057): 2272–81. https://doi.org/10.1016/S0140-6736(16)31279-X.

West, M., and J. Dawson. 2012. *Employee Engagement and NHS Performance.* London: King's Fund.

Wheeler, A. R. 2008. "Disconnecting the Stress-Burnout-Turnover Relationship Among Nursing Professionals: A Synthesis of Micro and Macro HRM Research." In *Handbook of Stress and Burnout in Health Care,* edited by J. R. B. Halbesleben, 187–99. New York: Nova Science Publishers.

Wiederhold, B. K., P. Cipresso, D. Pizzioli, M. Wiederhold, and G. Giuseppe. 2018. "Intervention for Physician Burnout: A Systematic Review." *Open Medicine* 13 (1): 253–63. https://doi. org/10.1515/med-2018-0039.

Winton, S., A. Cornelius, and M. Grawitch. 2022. "Providing Context to the Engagement-Behavior Linkage: A Facet-Level Examination." *Human Performance* 35 (1): 48–70. https://doi .org/1080/08959285.2021.1998062.

World Health Organization. 2020. *State of the World's Nursing 2020: Investing in Education, Jobs and Leadership.* Geneva: World Health Organization.

Wu, A. W., P. Buckle, E. R. Haut, T. Bellandi, S. Koizumi, A. Mair, J. Øvretveit, C. Power, H. Sax, E. J. Thomas, D. Newman-Toker, and C. Vincent. 2020. "Supporting the Emotional Well-Being of Health Care Workers During the COVID-19 Pandemic." *Journal of Patient Safety and Risk Management* 25 (3): 93–6. https://doi.org/10.1177/2516043520931971.

Yuan, C. T., E. H. Bradley, and I. M. Nembhard. 2015. "A Mixed Methods Study of How Clinician 'Super Users' Influence Others During the Implementation of Electronic Health Records." *BMC Medical Informatics and Decision Making* 15 (26): 1–10. https://doi.org/10.1186/s12911-015-0154-6.

Index

definition of, xvii, 31; disengagement component of, 31, 32, 34, 37, 62, 66; engagement related to: 49–52; exhaustion and, 31–32, 61, 62, 66; experience of, 31, 35; gender factors in, 34, 35; health affected by: 6–7; healthcare professional's perspective of: 8; health-related costs associated with: 11–12; as job dissatisfaction cause: 5; job performance affected by: 2–3; job turnover affected by: 5–6; as lack of motivation cause: 3; organizational performance affected by: 8–12; personal factors in: 34–35; prevention of: 93–94; protective factors against: 33–34; reduced professional efficacy in: 32; social support in reducing, 74, 95–97; stability of: 35–36; takeaway points: 36–37; turning point between stress and: 33; variables not linked to: 33–35; workflow affected by: 3–5

Burnout scores, variability in: 35

Canada, health-related costs in: 11
Cardiovascular disease, stress associated with: 6–7
CARES Act: 102–103
Challenges, identification of: 84–87
Change, improvement differentiated from, 90, 91
Clinical function, coordination of: 28
Clinical staff, stressors among: 23–27; patient demands: 24–25; working with other professionals: 26–27; working with technology: 27; workload, staffing, and scheduling: 25–26
Colleagues, as social support: 95–99

Commitment: in engagement, 41, 43, 65; lower, leading to turnover: 5; realistic job previews (RJPs) and: 103
Communication, among healthcare professionals: 26–27
Compassionate bundles: 108–109
Compassion fatigue: 24–25
Compensation: 107–108
Compensation, progressive, 101, 107
Conflict, work-family, 47–48, 104, 107
Conservation of resources theory, 20–22, 50, 64
Consideration, individualized: 78–79
Consultants, employees' relationships with: 77
Continuing education requirements: 106
Copenhagen Burnout Inventory: 62–63
Coping: active, 19, 21, 30; avoidant, 19, 21, 30, 36; with stress, xvii, 19, 21, 30, 36
Coronavirus Aid, Relief, and Economic Security (CARES) Act: 102–103
Costs, stress-related: 9–12
COVID-19 pandemic: xiii; American Rescue Plan Act and: 102–103; CARES Act and: 102–103; crisis management during: 109–111; family support for frontline workers during: 97; frontline managers during: 96–97; job turnover and: 5–6; organizational communication during: 99; patient demands during: 24–25; staffing shortages before: 5; staffing shortages during, xiii, 102–103; stress through perceived threat of: 20–21; walkrounds

during: 80; workload, staffing, and scheduling during: 25–26

Coworkers, support from: 96–97

Crew resource management training, 29, 90–91

Crisis management bundles: 109–111

Crossing the Quality Chasm (Institute of Medicine): 76

Cultural integration, of new employees: 105

Cynicism, 61, 62, 66

Data collection, in burnout reduction programs: 86–88

Dedication: 41

Deep breathing techniques: 70

Demerouti, Eva: 62

Depersonalization, 61, 62, 66

Developmental bundles: 100

Development programs: 106

Diabetes, stress associated with: 6–7

Disability claims: 12

Disengagement, 31, 32, 34, 37, 62, 66

Dissatisfaction, differentiated from stress: xv–xvi

Duke University: 80

Eating habits, stress associated with: 6–7

Efficacy, reduced personal: 32

Electronic health records (EHRs): 90

Emotional stress, patient care-related: 24

Emotional support: 96–97

Engagement: assessing, 57, 63–65; benefits of: 46–47; best approach to: 43–45; building, xiii, 39–56; burnout as parallel process to: 49–52; commitment in, 41, 43, 65; definitions of: 40–45; excessive: 47–49; fostering: 49–55; job crafting and: 48; job creativity

and: 48–49; performance, quality of care, patient safety and: 45–46; as practice: 42–43; qualities of: 41; resource caravans and: 52–54; resource investment and: 50; resource passageways and: 54–55; as a state of well-being: 41–42; takeaway points: 55–56; Utrecht Work Engagement Scale (UWES), 41–42, 43, 64; value of: 45–49; work–family conflict and: 48; of the workforce: 45–49

Environmental approaches, in burnout intervention, 70, 72–73

Errors, medical: accountability for: 29; effect of performance appraisals on: 107; reporting of, 13–14, 29, 83–84, 107

Evaluation: cognitive: xv; of crew resource management (CRM): 90–91; data collection for, 86–87, 90; for determining how to cope with stress: 19; employee performance evaluations: 98; "happy-sheet" approach in: 91; of individual-focused programs: 71–72

Exhaustion: 31; burnout caused by: 31–32; definition of: 31; disengagement leading to: 32; measuring, 61, 62, 66; professional efficacy and: 32

Expectations: feedback and: 43; management of, 88, 101, 103–104; misaligned or unmet, 5, 35, 103

Family–work conflict, 47–48, 104, 107

Feedback: to build relationships: 80; employees' access to, xviii, 43, 49, 54; in focus groups: 88; in performance appraisals: 106–107; for supportive environment: 98

Fight-or-flight response, 19, 32
Firefighting project, 73, 77–78, 84
Flex pools: 102
Flow: 41
Focus groups, 74, 75, 86–88, 120–121
Folkman, Susan: 18–20

Gallup Organization: 63–64
Gallup Q^{12}: 63–64
Gallup Workplace Audit: 63–64
Gender factors, in burnout, 34, 35

Health, adverse effects of burnout
    on: 6–7
Healthcare professionals: burnout
    from perspective of: 8; commu-
    nication among: 26–27; conse-
    quences of stress among: 2–8;
    flex pools and: 102; perspective
    of burnout among: 8; safety of:
    4; stress experienced by: xiii–xiv;
    stress-reducing interventions for:
    100–112; turnover rate among: 10;
    turnover replacement costs for:
    10; unmet expectations and: 103
Healthcare professions, turnover-
    related costs in: 9–11
Health-related costs of stress and
    burnout: 11–12
Hobfoll, Stevan, 20, 54
Human resources (HR) department,
    83–84, 99
Human resources management
    bundles: 100–111; compassionate
    bundles: 108–109; crisis manage-
    ment bundles: 109–111; stress-
    reducing bundles: 101–108
Hypotheses. *see* Theories

Ideas of others, taking an interest in:
    80–81
Identification in BRIDGES program,
    76, 81–88; of challenges: 84–87;

of opportunities, 76, 77, 89–91;
    of solutions: 87–88; of team
    members: 82–84; themes in: 85
Improvement, change differentiated
    from, 90, 91
Incompetence, stress differentiated
    from: xvi
Individualized consideration:
    78–79
Individualized interventions, xvii,
    70–72
Infertility, burnout as risk factor for:
    6
Information resources, for stress and
    burnout management: 113–117
Injuries: occupational, 4, 7, 103;
    workers' compensation claims
    for: 12
Institute of Medicine (IOM): *Cross-
    ing the Quality Chasm*: 76; qual-
    ity movement and: 28–29
International Disease Classification
    (ICD-11): xiii
Intervention programs: 57; failure
    of, xviii, 77; individualized, xvii,
    70–72; supportive work environ-
    ment-based: 95–99
Interviewing/interviews: in burnout
    reduction programs, 75, 79,
    80, 86, 87; interview form: 120;
    stress: 11

Jackson, Susan: 60
Job analysis, 101, 102, 106
Job applicants, realistic job previews
    (RJPs) for: 103–104
Job dissatisfaction, burnout-related: 5

Kahn, William, 41, 42, 43
Kerr, Steven: 98
Knowledge, skills, and abilities
    (KSAs), 106, 111–112
Kristensen, T. S.: 63

About the Author

Jonathon R. B. Halbesleben, PhD, is dean, Bodenstedt Chair, and Tom C. Frost Distinguished University Chair for Business Excellence of the Alvarez College of Business at the University of Texas at San Antonio. He is a fellow of the American Psychological Association and the Society for Industrial and Organizational Psychology.

Dr. Halbesleben has published more than 95 peer-reviewed articles based on his research on stress, burnout, engagement, and work–family relationships in such journals as the *Journal of Applied Psychology, Journal of Management, Medical Care, Medical Care Research and Review,* and *Health Care Management Review.* He is the editor of the *Handbook of Stress and Burnout in Health Care,* a scholarly compendium of current research on stress and burnout in the healthcare industry, and co-editor of *Research in Personnel and Human Resource Management,* an annual volume of research papers. He serves on the editorial boards of the *Academy of Management Review* and is former editor of the *Journal of Occupational and Organizational Psychology.* He has received research funding from the Agency for Healthcare Research and Quality, the National Institute for Occupational Safety and Health, the US Department of Defense, and the Centers for Disease Control and Prevention.

Dr. Halbesleben received his PhD and MS in industrial/organizational psychology from the University of Oklahoma and his BA in psychology from Winona State University. Prior to his position at the University of Texas at San Antonio, he held faculty positions at the University of Alabama, University of Wisconsin-Eau Claire, University of Missouri, and University of Oklahoma.

Dr. Halbesleben is married to his lovely wife, Jennifer Becker, and has three children, Alex, Liesl, and Oliver. He is a native of Wisconsin and enjoys running, Brewers baseball, Packers and Sooners football, and playing with his kids.